Forget That!

Books by Roger Flax

Forget That! 22 Lessons You Must Unlearn to Succeed
No Stopping You! How to Win the Game of Life

Roger Flax, PhD

Forget That!

22 Lessons You Must Unlearn to Succeed

BLACK STONE PUBLISHING

Published in 2025 by Blackstone Publishing
Cover and book design by Candice Edwards

Some names and identifying details have been changed to protect the privacy of individuals.

Printed in the United States of America

First edition: 2025
ISBN 979-8-8748-2162-3
Business & Economics / Business Communication / General

Version 1

Blackstone Publishing
31 Mistletoe Rd.
Ashland, OR 97520

www.BlackstonePublishing.com

I dedicate this book to the many very special people in my life who have taught me so many valuable lessons. Friends, teachers, colleagues, students, clients—you know who you are. Above all, my wonderful family—Judy, Kenny, Charlie, and Jonny. I owe you much more than thanks, and no words are adequate enough to describe what a blessing you are in my life. You inspire me every day. Love you guys a ton.

Mistakes made in life are our lessons in disguise. And sometimes, the best lessons learned came from the worst "mistakes made."

—Unknown

Contents

Preface

TIME TO DIG DEEP

When we were kids, we were like sponges.

We heard things for the very first time, and most of them sunk in. They sounded right and seemed to make sense. Invariably, we accepted them.

Well, at least many of them.

After all, we were new to the game of life, and what we heard was usually from family, adults we met, or so-called authorities. We were programmed to listen to our elders.

Incredibly, there were some things we were told only once in our lives, maybe for only five or ten seconds, that have stuck with us forever. And who knows if the person who told us knew what they were talking about? We were told, and for the most part, we believed. They knew what they were talking about, at least we assumed.

As we got older, we continued to hear new ideas, theories, and life principles that seemed logical and correct, and from purported authorities. So, we adopted them also. Most of them.

I certainly was guilty of this many times over.

Teachings from schoolteachers and instructors, college and graduate school professors, senior leaders, authors, and other "experts" who seemed to know what they were talking about.

Plus, our moms and dads were constantly teaching us life principles, whether we wanted to hear them. Ditto our grandparents, aunts, uncles, and trusted friends who always looked out for us. They all meant well in trying to help us.

But the questions remain: Was what they taught us correct? And have we ever questioned or challenged those things?

Specifically, was what we learned in school and beyond accurate and spot on, or were some of these teachings mistruths? Misinformation? Outright incorrect? Or somewhere in the middle?

Fast-forward to today, compound that confusion with the enormous, ongoing changes going on in this digital world we live in. With artificial intelligence potentially affecting almost everything and everyone, who knows where the world is headed?

But one thing is for sure. We live in a completely

different world than even five years ago. And if we don't correct the mistruths that were drilled into our heads years back, and adapt to these vast technological changes, we'll miss the boat and fall miles and miles behind.

That's the reality. That's life today.

EVER SINCE WE WERE KIDS . . .

We've been conditioned to listen to everything we were taught, good, bad, or indifferent.

Regardless of the background, experience, expertise, and knowledge of the person teaching us, most of these "Lessons to Unlearn" have stuck with us throughout our lives.

Even if the person advising or teaching us was clueless, unknowledgeable, or winging it about the subject matter, somehow a lot of what we heard became part of us.

And rarely, if ever, did we take the time to question or challenge these things, because they just seemed right.

The same thing happened regarding information we learned from books and published articles over the years. If it was published, it had to be correct. After all, an "expert" wrote it!

Many of these lessons learned over the years are simply not correct at all.

In fact, some are 100 percent wrong. They're the opposite of the truth, and diametrically opposed to what, in real life, is correct, what actually works. And what is truly factual and not just opinion.

Some of these lessons have led people to take ineffective actions, make poor decisions, and in some cases, encounter serious problems. These mistruths can handicap a person in their entire career and personal life.

It's time to take a serious look at these misperceptions, mistruths, and misleading falsehoods that have been in your head for years. And it's time to take action. It's time to forget them.

Keep in mind that this book isn't intended just for young adults trying to figure out how to become successful in their lives. It's also written for more experienced, savvy folks who might still be making the same mistakes repeatedly and wondering why.

WELCOME TO *FORGET THAT!* *22 LESSONS YOU MUST UNLEARN TO SUCCEED*

In this book, we'll look at these mistruths, misperceptions, and incorrect teachings . . . all that misinformation dumped on us. We'll unlearn them, once and for all, and get the misleading information out of our systems and out of our lives.

Evidence, research, and compelling examples will illustrate how incorrect, even dangerous, this misleading information can be.

You're about to read twenty-two chapters of old adages, rules, techniques, and principles. Twenty-two ideas that have rarely been challenged regarding their correctness, logic, and real-life applicability. You'll see plenty of examples of how these old adages are wrong.

After you see how senseless, irrelevant, and outdated some of this misinformation is, we'll convert all these mistruths into highly pragmatic, immediately applicable lessons. Specifically, real-life applications and recommended actions for you to take. You will learn solutions that contradict and resolve this nonsensical misinformation.

You may disagree with some of these points you're about to read. In fact, I hope you do, and challenge them.

But before you discard any of these corrections, think them through. Internalize them.

Think of your life and how these ideas apply, or do not apply. Think of examples in your past or present that justify what you're reading or oppose and negate them.

THE GOAL . . .

Dig deep. Challenge what you learned or were told. Gain refreshing, actionable new insights and

ideas—in your quest to become the most effective, action-oriented, successful person possible.

Many of the lessons to unlearn in this book are centered around work relationships and business, but you'll find them broadly applicable.

They can range from life's big picture . . . to relationships . . . to business communications . . . to family . . . to philosophies, proverbs, sayings, and quotations . . . to how-to tools and techniques.

THE FORMAT OF THE BOOK

Each chapter identifies a mistruth and demonstrates, through an example or two, the problem it creates. Then, you will be presented with what you should relearn, and how to apply these relearned concepts to real life. "Flaxseed Factors to Remember" will follow: This is a summary of the key action points to take with you and apply immediately. The final chapter ties all the lessons to unlearn into action steps and take-homes for you to ponder and apply.

Most of the names used for real-life examples in the book have been humorously contrived . . . to protect the author. But they're based on people I've encountered and their experiences with these mistruths.

I suggest you read this book multiple times, to let each individual lesson sink in and to see how each new concept might work for you. Space the readings a few weeks apart to give you time to digest and apply what you've learned into daily situations.

I want you to benefit greatly from the book and apply what you learn immediately. You will see and feel the impact and relevance as soon as you get started. Please let me know how you do with this new information.

Enjoy and be well. Here we go . . .

Part One
Reading People

Reading people—what an important skill this is. Why?

Some people feel that communication is the key skill needed to be mastered to be successful in business and everyday life. Although they might be correct, the skill that is the true foundation of effective communication is reading people.

When you know how to read people, it affects almost every aspect of your life, personally and professionally. When you have read the other person and their communication style well, you're off to a head start in establishing trust and a good relationship with them. If you misread them, and the way they communicate, it can lead to problems, frustrations, and a dead-end relationship.

Effective communication with others starts with

your ability to ascertain what they're thinking and how they feel. Gaining insight into those two areas can help you identify and solve problems, establish rapport with others, and motivate, inspire, and influence them.

At the core of reading people is power listening, also called active listening.

You've heard repeatedly how important it is to be a good listener, and it's no doubt the key to reading people quickly and accurately. Specifically, listening to their words, tone of voice, nonverbal signals, implications, and what they don't say but imply.

Good, active listening enables you to read all of those messages and helps build trust and rapport. Even if you don't quite comprehend what the person is verbally saying, decoding and understanding their facial expressions will give you relevant insights as to what they want to say but aren't saying.

It's important to unlearn some of the many reading-people mistruths we have heard and adopted over the years. This section focuses on five specific lessons to unlearn immediately.

One
Lesson to Unlearn #1
Treat All People the Same

Absolutely not! Forget that!

No two people are exactly the same. Each is different in one way or another or in many ways.

That's why you can't treat all people the same. It simply won't work and will come back to haunt you sooner or later, probably sooner.

Take these six acquaintances of mine who are all good people but are totally different:

One doesn't stop talking; he goes on and on all day and all night if you let him. At meetings, once he starts, it's hard to stop him. That's why many people skip his meetings or nod off. He probably talks in his sleep.

The second one is the quietest, shyest, least comfortable person imaginable . . . but a terrific human being, very credible and extremely articulate when she finally does speak. Everyone in her company respects her and what she has to say, when you get it out of her.

A third acquaintance is a wonderful, giving person, but the world's biggest know-it-all. There's no topic he's not an expert in, and even when he has limited knowledge about a subject, he pretends just the opposite and spouts out information. His facts are usually opinions.

The fourth person interrupts you whenever you're speaking. Doesn't matter where you are in the sentence or what you're speaking about. He dives in and offers his opinion, even when unasked. And you can tell while you're speaking that he's thinking about what he wants to say.

The fifth person is clearly in another world while you're speaking. It's obvious that he's daydreaming or waiting for you to finish talking so he can dive in.

The sixth person represents the most common example of them all. He might be honest and forthright, but he exaggerates and stretches the truth ad nauseam. There's no telling what's true and what's BS coming out of his mouth. And as you might predict, his credibility is, at best, borderline. Lots of people in this world are just like him.

All six of these people are solid human beings but totally different.

There is absolutely no way you can treat them all the same. It just won't work. A particular communication style that works with one individual might backfire with the next.

There are dozens of other examples we can all come up with about varying types of people with different traits and characteristics.

Each person feels equally important in their mind. They have their own dreams, needs, wants, goals, objectives . . . and to each of them, these items might be the most important things in their lives.

Each person also has their own personality and communication style. That's why you can't communicate with each of them the very same way. It just doesn't work.

Let's take a look.

FOUR DIFFERENT PERSONALITY STYLES OF PEOPLE

In general, most people possess one of these four personality styles: passive, passive-aggressive, assertive, and aggressive.

A **passive** person usually avoids expressing their opinions and inner feelings. They hold them in, usually too much. They often don't protect their rights or fully identify and meet their needs.

When this builds up too much, they're like a bubble that bursts. They treat the frustration even more irrationally than they should and, subsequently, are ashamed or feel guilty about their ugly outburst.

A **passive-aggressive** person might come across passively and superficially might react in an accepting manner. Don't always buy that because deep inside, they can be irritated, frustrated, and angry. Their facial expressions, nonverbal gestures, and tone of voice don't always reflect how they truly feel internally.

They can become sarcastic yet powerless in expressing themselves. They rarely take responsibility for their own actions and pass blame to others for their mistakes.

An **assertive** person confidently and decisively shares their opinions and usually lets you know exactly how they feel, without necessarily offending you or putting you off. They disagree when necessary and know how to say no. They're usually good listeners who speak more calmly and thoughtfully and try to connect with others. They feel good about themselves, and people sense that. They make friends easily.

An **aggressive** person directly and clearly expresses their feelings and needs, usually in a loud, forceful way, and often tries to dominate others. They can be amoral or thin-skinned and not take constructive criticism well, and can be quickly angered or defensive when they don't like what they hear.

They're not active listeners and rudely interrupt people repeatedly. They can be intimidating, daunting, hurtful, and never admit to being wrong. They might say, "I'm fine" or "I'm OK," but their tone of voice, intonation, and volume speak the total opposite.

Which one of these styles is you? Think about the people you deal with most frequently, personally and at work. Which one of these styles describes them?

Stop for a minute, choose five or six people you know quite well, and give some thought to which personality they represent.

Each person has their own style, and embedded within that style are varying ways they act, behave, and respond to other people.

All people are distinctive in their own way and have differing needs, behaviors, hot buttons, and WIIFMs. WIIFM stands for "What's in it for me."

Yes, you should treat each person with the same level of respect and understanding. But to treat each person the same way is a mistake and a terrible habit to get into. It can create unnecessary, serious interpersonal relationship problems.

Why?

Since everybody is different, one interpersonal communication style you demonstrate might work effectively with one person but could explode with another.

Your boss or supervisor is different from your peers, and your peers are different from your reports, associates, and customers.

Everybody's got their own quirks, idiosyncrasies, nuances, securities, insecurities, hang-ups, whatever. That's the world around us.

And because of that fact of life, once and for all, you must realize that you can't treat all people the same.

FIRST, TRY READING EACH PERSON'S COMMUNICATION TYPE

Now that you understand the four general personality types, learning how to effectively and quickly read people can be a huge asset. Specifically, identify their communication style and use that to figure out how to connect with them.

THE RPQ TECHNIQUE: READING PEOPLE QUICKLY . . . AND ACCURATELY

Reading people quickly (RPQ) is an effective, simple technique to identify a person's communication style so you can connect with them.

Remember: Communicate based on who they are and how they communicate, not who you are and how you feel comfortable communicating.

Most people do the opposite. They communicate the same way to other people, regardless of how the other person comes across and communicates themselves.

This rule goes for everybody, including your bosses, subordinates, friends, spouses, family members, in-laws, outlaws, best friends, biggest enemies, greatest admirers . . . name it.

Here's how you quickly read the other person's

communication style and adapt your style, accordingly, applying the RPQ tool:

The moment you meet the person, listen to them carefully, study them, and ask yourself these three RPQ questions . . .

Question #1: Are they a "speaker" or "listener"? Do they seem to enjoy doing the speaking and dominating the conversation? If so, then let them do most of the speaking, ask questions, and stay on their track. Don't switch to yours.

The **"speaker"** usually wants to do all the speaking and invariably control and even bulldoze the conversation. If you try to interrupt them while they're speaking, watch out! That could be a quick dealbreaker.

The **"listener"** prefers to listen rather than speak and speaks only when necessary. They know the value and benefits of listening and enjoy it more than speaking. You've got to communicate with them differently than the "speaker," who can ramble on all day if you permit them.

Question #2: Are they a "me" or a "you" person? That's pretty easy to determine. Just listen carefully to see if they use the words "me" or "I" frequently, or the word "you" more than "me" or "I." Ascertain whether they center the conversation around themselves, or around you.

The "me" person loves speaking about themselves

and all they've accomplished or are involved in. If you counted the number of times they said "I," the number would be staggering.

The "you" person has genuine interest in hearing about you, and not speaking about themselves. However, if you notice that characteristic but try getting them to talk about themselves more, you might actually be annoying them without realizing it, and be perceived as being manipulative.

At a recent client meeting, the administrative assistant asked me about my family. Nice of her to do so. But the moment I started telling her about my three sons, she hijacked the conversation, got up, and quickly showed me pictures of her four children and eight grandkids. Oh well!

Question #3: Are they a "results" person or a "relationship" person? The "results" person is easy to spot. They want to get right down to business and hear the value and relevance of your proposition or ideas. You should quickly get to the point after a brief introduction, state your supporting facts and details, conclude, and welcome questions.

If you start schmoozing with them, they may cordially ask you to curtail that to a later time and get to the heart of why you're meeting together.

The "relationship" person is just the opposite. They

enjoy developing a relationship first, or at least establishing a comfortable rapport, before jumping into the meeting's business segment. They usually don't mind if you slow down a bit and learn more about each other's background before the actual business discussion begins.

The "relationship" person is usually not in as much of a hurry as the "results" person is. So, your strategy should be to gauge the situation, possibly take your time at the outset of the meeting, and try developing trust, rapport, and positive feelings with the person.

If you misread their style and move away from the rapport-building stage of the meeting and abruptly segue into the business conversation, they might get offended and put off. They also might think that your sole purpose is to eagerly make a sale and not develop a sound relationship with them.

Among the many real-life examples gathered during my career over the years, I have experienced four that have stood out. Two positive examples with good outcomes, and two negative examples that led to disappointing outcomes.

Example #1: Allan Sands loved to talk about himself and abhorred listening to people speak. He faked attention and constantly interrupted people.

The first day I met him, during a proposal meeting, I quickly realized that he had no real interest in hearing me propose an idea. I could see that signal in his body language in around seven seconds.

But Allan's boss had requested that I give him a thirty-minute presentation on a business idea I had for them. I had to do this even though this represented a potential dilemma.

So, what did I do? I opened the meeting graciously with an attention-getting "grabber" to stimulate his immediate interest, stating my objective for the session, and asking him a few questions.

And for the entire time, Allan didn't stop talking about himself and all he knew about the subject at hand. I couldn't treat him the same way I treated people who were genuinely interested in what I had to say. If I had interrupted his nonstop speaking, it would have offended him.

Finally, after his endless rambling, he gazed at his watch, told me to give him my proposal, and let him know what I wanted.

I did that in around ninety seconds. He nodded his head, asked me two short questions, and exclaimed, "I like it, sounds very good, let's do a pilot program."

I conducted the pilot program, and that eventually led to two decades of work with him, his organization, his people, and their successors. I attribute this great business success to initially reading his communication style and adapting mine to his.

Allan was clearly a SPEAKER-ME-RESULTS person. Who knows what would have happened if I had turned the communication from him doing all the speaking to me jumping in to talk?

Example #2: Rick Borpup, 180 degrees different from Allan Sands, detested speaking to groups, even small ones with three or four people sitting around a conference table.

Rick was also a hyper, fidgety person and didn't like to be at meetings that lasted longer than fifteen minutes. He was uncomfortable talking about himself.

I could have done the same thing with Rick as I did with Allan. But instead, I acknowledged how busy he was and that I really appreciated him giving me some of his valuable time.

I quickly proposed a few ideas, and he bought one of them, and boom, we had a tentative deal.

Had I facilitated him to speak about himself and his needs too much, he would have probably escorted me to the exit and written me off in seconds. In fact, he mentioned to me that he liked my clear, direct, to-the-point style.

Quite frankly, I did nothing to earn that compliment. I just read his communication style and got to the point. Rick was a LISTENER-YOU-RESULTS person.

Rick and Allan were in many aspects total opposites. I never could have treated them the same way because it would have blown up in my face.

Incidentally, Rick is still a major client, and a close friend of mine. Nevertheless, I must dominate or at least lead the conversation versus sitting back and just listening to him. Otherwise, there'd be uncomfortable, dead silence. He simply isn't a speaker, and facilitating him to do more speaking might be perceived as manipulation.

Example #3: Chuck Beveridge hated meetings and loved red wine. He didn't take himself too seriously and loved to have fun. Far from being a serious businessperson, his goal was to minimize his work hours as much as possible.

So, my game plan with Chuck was to meet outside the office or on the tennis courts and talk about very little business while playing. His personality lent itself to all play and no work.

I simply followed the prescription and treated him like a buddy, not a client, with all kinds of fun things to do during the day and after work. All tied into the business, but fun shadowed work.

Obviously, Chuck was a SPEAKER-ME-RELATIONSHIP guy. And he adored a Lamborghini red.

Example #4: Matt Majors was a good client but didn't like to meet face-to-face with people.

Zoom was a godsend for Matt, and having remote meetings instead of in-person ones was the best thing that ever happened to him. He could wear a sports jacket on the top half of his body and sweatpants on the bottom because nobody knew and Zoom meetings allowed that attire.

He preferred to keep his meetings quick and efficient. Remote meetings let him talk without needing to chitchat before or after.

Although Relationship Building 101 preaches that you should meet important clients in person periodically, and not just over the phone or Zoom, I still, to this day, have never been in the same room with Matt, and we're doing a lot of business together.

Matt's communication style is SPEAKER-ME-RESULTS. I adapted my communication style to his, and we're doing just fine working together.

All four of these people were good, talented people, but all were totally different from the others.

And I was totally different in my communication style with each one of them, basing it on my perception of their initial communication style.

The key is to read people quickly, and then act appropriately based on who they are and what you perceive their communication style is . . . not who you are and how you want to communicate your message.

Unlearn the lesson learned right now. That is, to treat all people the same. It's a fallacy. Forget that!

APPLYING THIS TO REAL LIFE

Try doing this today and from now on. It's easy if you simply make up your mind to do so.

When you meet a new person, first listen, be cordial and respectful, then begin to apply the reading people quickly technique.

Listen to them and determine if they're a "speaker" who enjoys talking a lot and grabbing center stage or a "listener" who seems to be a bit quieter or reserved, and more interested in you doing the speaking.

Then, keep note if they're a "me" or "you" person. If they're a "me" person, let them keep talking about themselves and steer the conversation away from you. Just keep in mind the main objective of the conversation.

And finally, are they results/bottom-line-oriented and want to get to the point (a "results" person) . . . versus a relationship person who wants to take their time, get to know you a bit . . . and then dive into business?

This initial process should take only a minute or two, but you'll quickly ascertain who they are when communicating. Plus, their body language is telling. You can read the other person's communication style and adapt your style to theirs.

That'll give you a head start in developing what could be a solid relationship with them. It's powerful and works like magic every time.

This morning, playing tennis with people I hadn't previously known, we talked a few minutes before the match, and I quickly realized that the other guy was a LISTENER-YOU-RELATIONSHIP person. But his doubles partner, who rambled on profusely when we first met, was clearly a SPEAKER-ME-RESULTS person, and I let him talk, talk, talk . . . and it seemed to work.

We had solid chemistry from the get-go, good communication, and had a great time playing. My gut feeling was that a good relationship had been born, and we already had a tentative exploratory business meeting set up. It all started with applying the RPQ technique.

And regarding the other person, I had an exploratory meeting with senior partners of a law firm who had expressed interest in my working with their firm as a communication consultant. We performed the RPQ technique with each of the partners, and we had a mutually beneficial first discussion with excellent chemistry.

One of the lawyers, a "speaker," didn't stop talking throughout the entire meeting. The other two lawyers were listeners, so I had to adapt my style to theirs, and ask questions to get them to speak a little. But it worked out fine. It usually does.

Always remind yourself that the way we approach people shouldn't be where we are at, but where they are at. Proceed from there and watch what happens.

It's a falsehood that you should treat all people the same. If you have done that over the years, beginning today, please don't. Use RPQ—it truly works.

FLAXSEED FACTORS TO REMEMBER

1. No two people are the same.

2. Approach each person as if they are different from anyone else. Don't approach people from where you are at; approach them from where they are at.

3. In general, people fit into one of the following four personality types: passive, passive-aggressive, assertive, and aggressive.

4. Read the communication style of each person you meet, analyze their type, and adapt yourself and your communication style to the way they are, not the way you feel like acting.

5. The reading people quickly (RPQ) technique helps you adapt your style to that person based on their style. Are they a "speaker" or "listener" person? Are they a "me" or "you" person? Are they a "results" person or a "relationship" person?

6. Treat people the way they will value and appreciate. And put yourself in their shoes.

Two

Lesson to Unlearn #2

Most People Are Honest and Tell You the Truth

This is a sensitive topic! And where you might say that I'm off base.

Why? Because most people are good human beings. They are basically honorable, and usually speak the truth.

But most people also stretch the truth, or lie, or occasionally tell a "little white lie" about small, unimportant matters that nobody really cares about.

Or they have hidden agendas. They say one thing, but their real purpose and ulterior motive is another. Borders on being a bit dishonest.

I'll bet you somebody has lied to you this week, and chances are, you've lied or stretched the truth with somebody this week. Not serious, "criminal" lies . . . but stretching the truth a bit or exaggerating.

We all tell little white lies periodically, and that's

normal. We want to protect ourselves or another person, which might be necessary at that time. An outright, blatant lie might just protect ourselves and avoid a potential problem or confrontation.

Millions of people are guilty of this. Well, the word, "guilty" might be a little strong; let's change it to . . . millions of people do this.

It's key that you are tuned into this trait of most people. Not that you're going to disown them and your relationship. But you'll be a step or two ahead of them.

Check out this lie, or to be precise, a $1,100 saga . . .

My car had a coffee holder on the dashboard, and for two years, the holder wouldn't close. I tried to jam it, hit it, pry it shut, joggle with the connecting parts, you name it. A real pain in the neck.

I asked other people to help me close the jammed coffee holder, but none could do it without potentially breaking it. Zero results. It was clearly mangled, and no non-handyman like me would ever be able to unmangle it.

So, when I received my five-thousand-mile car tune-up, I asked the service rep, Rip Offski, to take a look at the coffee holder and see if he could fix it while he tuned up my car.

When I returned a few hours later, Rip, who seemed like the most sincere, diligent guy in the world, told me some bad news.

"We cannot close the dispenser and must take apart

the entire dashboard to go inside and find out the cause of this problem." When I asked what that would cost me, he said give or take $1,100, depending upon how long it took them.

"Are you kidding me?" I exclaimed. And that was just to fix my silly coffee holder.

I thanked Rip and told him I'd think about it. Turns out, that would be the last time I'd ever have anything to do with him, or the dealership. Tearing apart my entire car dashboard to fix a tiny dispenser. Damn.

When I drove out of the service area, I put my fingers inside the holder one more time, dug down deep, and felt a napkin, hard as a rock, stuck at the base of the dispenser. Hmm!

When I stuck my fingernail under the rock-solid, coffee-stained napkin, I removed it. Then I tried closing the dispenser, and shockingly and magically, it closed easily. Like nothing at all was the matter. It worked perfectly.

Turns out there was no problem at all—just a two-year-old rotten napkin frozen on the base of the dispenser. And four seconds for me to remove it.

What might have cost me over a grand, and several days of dropping off my car, cost me nothing except four seconds of my time trying to fix it myself. And when I called the serviceman, Rip Offski, and told him what had just happened, there was dead silence.

I never ever went back there. And never plan to. This is a great example of people stretching the truth. And it could have been a very expensive one.

A second example could have been astronomically costly, and reinforces the mistruth that people are basically honest. Sadly, they are not.

I needed major dental surgery. X-rays showed that I needed two implants to fix my problem. An implant, if you don't know, is a medical device that's surgically inserted into the jaw to restore a person's ability to chew and improve their appearance. Implants support crowns, dentures, and bridges. And they cost tons of money.

My dentist told me that he wasn't that experienced in performing implants and the major dental surgery needed. I admired him for that because he could have made at least $4,000 or so for the work.

So, I contacted two dental surgeons to assess what I needed and the costs. The first told me that his fee was $45,000 for the implant and related surgery. But he also said that I would first have to see his colleague, a general dentist, who would examine and work on that area of my mouth to remove any potential decays, cavities, infections, etc.

He referred me to a dentist who, after examining me for around twelve minutes, told me that I needed a great deal of "prep" work before the implant to prepare me for the upcoming surgery.

"Doc, what will that cost me?" I asked him. He left the examining room, went to his computer, and came back with an astounding $35,000 cost.

Shocked and on the verge of getting depressed over his costs, I told him that between his $35K and the dental surgeon's $45K, it would cost me $80,000 for the work. I asked him if he could do any better with the price, and he abruptly said, "No, do you have any idea what my overhead is?"

I decided to shop around and speak to other well-known and successful general dentists and implant specialists. I saw a periodontist and general dentist, both with good reputations, who assessed my problem differently than the first pair of dentists and quoted me $40,000. This was still a hefty amount but half of what the other two dentists had quoted me.

I decided to get one more consultation regarding my problem and saw a third set of doctors. Incidentally the three separate twenty-minute consultations from these dentists ranged from $450 to $1,700 per consult, for the exact same examination, X-rays, and assessment. The second consultation was four times the cost of the first one, and the work was exactly the same.

That third dentist assessed my problem and agreed to $18,000. He referred me to a dental surgeon whom he strongly recommended and said, "He is the best in the field at implant surgery." That doctor proposed to do the work for $7,500.

A grand total of $25,500 for the entire implant job. Not shabby, but compare that to the original $80,000 proposal! This is just another example of how people are not necessarily honest. One of those docs no doubt was hosing me, and thankfully I did my homework before diving into the work.

HOW DO YOU SEE THROUGH THIS KIND OF STUFF?

Not easily.

It's never a simple task to figure out when a person isn't telling it like it is. With digital communication so prevalent, it's harder than ever to detect falsehood; when a person emails, you can't read their body language or hear their tone of voice.

There are some things to look out for that can help you guard yourself:

1. The old adage "It's not what a person says, but how they say it" holds true here. If they are communicating in person or on Zoom or

Teams meetings, listen to their tone of voice and carefully observe their body language. Both are extremely telling and give you clear signals that something's just not right.

2. The person adds a bunch of "I thinks, "I believes," or "I feels" when you ask challenging questions. Especially if the person has previously come across confidently and decisively, it's a hint that something isn't true when they start to mumble these weak words.

3. The annoying, distracting "Um," "Uh," "Hmm," "Ah," "Well," and other meaningless filler words begin to surface. When these unwords suddenly appear, take notice.

4. The person says, "OK," "Ya know," or "Right," at the end of a sentence or even in the middle. This is a red flag.

5. Restating the question or declarative statement when it is unnecessary to do so. This can be a stalling tactic geared to buy time or defuse previous words. Example: "Did you think I did that? Of course, I did not."

6. Watch for someone who avoids contractions, which most people use naturally. "I have never done that" versus "I've never done that."

7. Resorting to hackneyed, weak expressions such as "To be perfectly honest with you," or "To tell you the truth," or "The fact of the matter is," or "Seriously, I would never ever do that."

8. Hedging their responses. "As far as I can recall," or "What I recollect is."

9. "I never received your email" has risen to number one in the "World Lie Survey." How many times has somebody told you, "I never got your email. Probably got lost in cyberspace." Yeah, right!

APPLYING THIS TO REAL LIFE

As I mentioned earlier, most people lie but don't mean anything criminally offensive by it. They're just stretching the truth, or not telling it like it is.

Don't become cynical after reading this chapter or look for the negatives in people or be constantly evaluating and assessing them. Instead, be aware of the fact that people don't always tell the truth. Even family members who love and cherish you. Sometimes, they stretch the truth, cover up, or lie to protect themselves.

That is human nature.

So how do you recognize a lie?

Reread the above section and incorporate that kind of thinking all the time when you deal with others. Note tone of voice and body language such as shoulder shrugging, distant or no expression, sudden fidgeting like playing with their hair or pressing their fingers to their cheeks.

Also note their eye contact. Are they looking elsewhere and not going eye to eye with you?

Finally, if you're communicating with others via email or text, see if they're vague with their answers or complicating things unnecessarily or sidestepping challenging questions or issues.

Trust your gut feelings and intuition. People might lie to you a bit, but your heart never does.

FLAXSEED FACTORS TO REMEMBER

1. Most people are forthright and honorable for the most part, but sometimes stretch the truth, exaggerate, tell white lies, and on occasion, tell blatant lies.

2. Don't become cynical about this. Acknowledge it, accept it, and learn to deal with it.

3. People often have an ulterior motive.

4. Remind yourself of the powerful expression, "It's not what you say, but how you say it." Carefully observe tone of voice and body language. Listen to what people say but note how they say it. Listen "between the lines" for hidden messages and hints.

5. Listen for filler words. Examples are "Uh," "Um," "Err," "Ah," "Ya know," "OK," and "Well." And listen for phrases that try to stall, distract, or cover up. Listen for facts and examples versus opinions, false inferences, or generalizations.

6. Despite all this, look for the positives in people, not the negatives.

Three

Lesson to Unlearn #3

There Are Two Sides to Every Story

Forget that! That's not the case in most situations.

You've heard the "two sides to every story" expression since you were a child. And you probably hear it frequently today, especially when two people are in a heated argument, disagreement, or debate or are telling you their side of the story.

But the "two sides to every story" adage is usually untrue. It's centuries old and totally outdated.

There are often two different versions of ostensibly the same event. Not just two sides.

This adage might date back to the mid-eighteenth century. But the concept itself comes from an ancient fable that goes back to the Greek writer Aesop (620–564 BCE).

Aesop wrote in the fable "The Mule" that every

truth has two sides. Well, things have changed a bit since the days of Aesop.

The late, great film producer Robert Evans, who produced legendary films like *Urban Cowboy* and *Chinatown*, and who was the head of production at Paramount during the making of *The Godfather*, *Rosemary's Baby*, and *Love Story*, vehemently once said:

"There are three, not two sides to every story: yours, mine, and the truth."[1]

That was spot on, Bob, and very insightful.

We often assume there are two sides, two accounts to every story when two people argue, strongly disagree, or are "miles apart" with their explanation of who is right. One person is right, and the other is wrong—at least that's how it appears.

Or when we, ourselves, strongly disagree with what a person is telling us, and our argument and rationale is diametrically opposed to theirs.

The truth is . . . there are rarely two sides to every story. There usually are three.

*Person A's side . . .

*Person B's side . . . and

*Person C's side . . . that "invisible" person who exists somewhere in between the other two and knows or represents the truth.

Person A is absolutely convinced about their account or justification of something . . . what they saw, felt, or strongly believed. They give their account of it, their side of the discussion, disagreement, or argument. How they saw it. Often, they give "half-truths."

Person B gives a completely different account or side of the same discussion, disagreement, or argument. How they saw it. How sure they are. "Half-truths," once again.

And the two of them, amazingly, are night and day apart with their explanations . . . but both are fervently emphatic about their thoughts. Both are insistent that they're totally correct.

Hard to believe they both witnessed the same thing or discussed the same issue.

Well, somewhere in between, **Person C**, is where the real truth lies.

And although both parties are absolutely positive of what the truth is, neither is usually 100 percent correct. That's the way human nature is.

We frequently stretch the truth a bit. Sometimes even a lot.

We often see things the way we want to see them. And we perceive things the way we want to perceive them. Same thing goes with listening.

A study once showed that 60 percent of people surveyed admitted lying or stretching the truth in a ten-minute conversation.

They want to make their point, so they stretch or bend the truth. Enter that invisible Person C.

FOUR REAL-LIFE EXAMPLES

Four examples clearly back up the "three sides to every story" premise.

1. **Vera Shor** was adamant about what she felt—that the company's CEO played favorites giving senior-level promotions.

"The dynamic, charismatic, pushier people," she felt," always get the big jobs." Didn't matter what substance and expertise they provided—their fluff, charisma, and aggressiveness paved the way. Vera was positive about the CEO's behavior and style of promoting people. No doubt in her mind.

The CEO, Frank Leaderman, vehemently opposed Vera's accusation. He was astounded at her misperceptions. He unequivocally said her argument was fantasy and sour grapes.

"Style means very little to me, not much at all," Frank said, "because expertise, proven track record, and interpersonal skills are what I look for in a person. And I don't appreciate pushy, overly aggressive people!"

The two of them were 180 degrees apart. Somewhere in the middle, person C represented the truth. That was the consensus of most employees.

---

2. **Manny Faxit**, newly appointed vice president of a major manufacturing company, heard "confidentially" from several senior managers that his budget would be reduced by around 20 percent.

Note the quotation marks around the word "confidentially" because almost nothing these days is ever kept totally confidential. And social media has exacerbated the problem. But keeping things confidential covers another lesson to unlearn we'll get to later.

Manny's boss, Bernie Outz, said that budget cuts weren't at all what he (Bernie) said.

"The budget's basically remaining the same. That's a rumor you're hearing, Manny, so get over it," Bernie said.

These two people had completely opposite viewpoints.

Somewhere in the middle is the truth of what was spoken. And Manny is still wondering and stressed-out as to how big the cuts will be, and where his future lies.

---

3. The **car dealership example** is classic. Carmen DePinto had decided to purchase a new car, and purportedly had the following dialogue with Justin Lyze, the dealership's sales manager.

Carmen (potential purchaser):

"You clearly told my husband and me the other day

that we could pay off the car in three installments over six months. And now you've changed your pitch and are demanding we give you a 50 percent down payment and pay the remaining balance within thirty days."

Justin Lyze (the sales manager) responded:

"With all due respect, Mrs. DePinto, I'm positive I didn't say that."

Keep track of the number of times you hear the words "due respect" in a week. It's almost as trite as the words "that being said" or "to be perfectly honest with you."

"What I said was for you to give me a deposit of 10 percent now and pay the rest when you pick up the car. I'm positive I said that," Justin stated.

Neither person would budge, and Carmen walked out disgusted.

Both people were 100 percent positive of what they said. Hard to believe. The words "being positive" can often mean "I'm pretty sure . . ."

Somewhere in the middle of Carmen and Justin's two arguments, and most people's arguments, lies the truth. Sadly, that's the way people are, and always have been.

---

4. I have a **client** who told me for years that her husband had a vile temper and threatened her repeatedly.

Very sad story. One time, she said she had to call the police to protect herself.

But I met her husband years later, and he told me that his ex-wife had a horrific temper and punched him repeatedly when she was angry (and a bit smashed).

Go figure!

I learned this mistruth of "two sides to every story" when I was a young kid.

I'll never forget when I was around six, my buddy Cliff Sauer told me that his sister, Jenny, was always hiding his baseball glove. She denied it. Jenny, meanwhile, told me that Cliff was a big jerk because he was always hiding her favorite doll. He denied that also.

Both swore to me they were positive as to what the other kid had done, and I listened to both sides, even though I couldn't care less. Somewhere in the middle must have been the truth.

I subsequently overheard their mom telling her husband that she hid Cliff's glove because all he did was play baseball, day and night, and never did his homework. And she hid Jenny's doll because she (Jenny) was obsessed with it. But both kids swore their side of the story about the other kid was 100 percent true.

In sum, never assume that there are two sides to every story—there usually are three, and that's where the real truth lies. "Person C" exists everywhere in our lives.

It's important to look at or hear both sides of an argument objectively because it's likely you'll eventually hear all or most of the facts and be able to draw your own conclusions.

APPLYING THIS TO REAL LIFE:

How do you dig deep? Use the simple acronym PDC as the mental model to employ:

P: Look for each person's main idea and overall **purpose (P)** or objective. Look for their main point of disagreement or contention. Don't stop searching for it until you get it.

D: Ask them to support it with evidence—facts, **details (D)**, data, or examples. Probe for the accuracy and impact of this supporting information. Separate their facts from their opinions. Ask questions and carefully study their body language and tone of voice.

C: Draw your own **conclusions (C)**.

This process may sound a bit arduous, but it isn't at all. It will become natural for you once you get in the habit of doing it when other people try to convince you of something. It takes only a few moments to do—but you'll usually obtain the real truth. And isn't that your ultimate goal?

Be skeptical, not cynical, when you hear two people disagreeing or debating, and assuring you they're right. Or two people trying to convince you of something, but each has a different story.

Not to say you should be a skeptical person in general. But there's nothing wrong with being somewhat on guard—so many people stretch the truth. When people have their sides of the story, take your time and probe into what the real story is, knowing it could be somewhere in the middle.

And when you're confronted by that situation, do the same analysis yourself—PDC.

FLAXSEED FACTORS TO REMEMBER

1. There usually aren't two sides to every story. There are three. Person A, Person B, and somewhere in the middle of them, that invisible, infamous Person C, the truth.

2. People often omit or stretch the truth. Some do it intentionally; some do it subconsciously. Sadly, most people do it one way or the other, a fact of life.

3. Always dig deep and probe when you hear two people debating or arguing over a point of contention. Find that third person.

4. As a rule, don't necessarily accept what you hear when people tell you something. Question it.

5. If you don't dig deep, you'll probably jump to a false conclusion, or act on a mistruth.

6. Like my earlier book, *No Stopping You! How to Win the Game of Life* emphasized . . . "In life, you may lose many of the battles and still win the war." The battles go away; they disappear. The war is the big picture, the overall strategy and plan, and has serious meaning. Lose some battles in life. In the long run, you'll probably be glad you did.

7. Go for "win-win" outcomes. They are usually best for everyone.

Four

Lesson to Unlearn #4

Believe People When They Say: "I Know for a Fact" or "I'm 99.9 Percent Sure!"

How many times a week do you hear people say, "I know for a fact." Or even worse, "**Trust me**, I know for a fact."

Forget that! Watch out for those words when you hear them.

They are usually said because the person is either insecure or unconfident about what they're saying. Or they're insecure in general, with little or no confidence in themselves. Or they're basically "full of it" and like to hear themselves talk.

Or they're simply not telling the truth.

People use the opening "I know for a fact" a lot. Just to sell something or make their point. And the funny thing is that it's usually not a fact at all. It's often an opinion they feel strongly about so they call it a fact. Sometimes they say it so much that they're totally unaware they're saying it.

Even parents, trying to convince their kids of something, often use the "trust me, I know for a fact" declaration. Does that mean that they shouldn't be trusted or believed?

Do you have a habit of saying it? If so, it's not helping your cause. It might even hurt it, but most people won't tell you. Start noticing if people say it, or if you say it yourself.

Hugh Mongiss "quoted" to friends what his doctor purportedly told him—

"Trust me, I know for a fact . . . that proactively taking a statin every day will keep my cholesterol under control. I spoke to my nationally renowned internist, and he assured me that although you really don't need to take statins unless your cholesterol is dangerously high, taking it daily will help control your cholesterol level!"

Let's examine closely the point that Mr. Mongiss tried to make, and the hyperbole he used.

A. Did he, himself, thoroughly review the research on statins, and find that research studies clearly indicate that a person should take X milligrams of a statin daily to keep their cholesterol down?

B. Is his "nationally renowned" internist truly nationally renowned? Who says? Does everybody around the country know of this apparent expert?

> Have they read his journal articles? Has he written any? What are the background facts about him?

People spout off information like this without truly thinking about what they are saying and what the possible repercussions might be. They speak from the hip.

Is what they're saying totally factual, or is it important data but not 100 percent verified? Or are they just dangerously using the word "fact" to sound positive and convincing?

Each time you come out with mistruths like this, you lose your credibility and trust with people a little more.

And if people don't believe you in this statement, how can they believe you in anything else you say or profess, even if it's true?

Here's another example of a person misusing the word "fact."

"Trust me, I know for a fact that the car accident was his fault. He went right through the stop sign."

Did the person see a video of it, or are there witnesses who saw the incident firsthand?

Again, this is an example of overuse of the statement, "I know for a fact," and the "trust me" words that can be perceived as hype. Also, an example of not separating fact from opinion.

Using these phrases is a dangerous habit, and an

important lesson to unlearn. If what you are saying is genuinely a fact, you don't have to say, "I know for a fact." Just state the fact.

Saying "trust me" raises red flags and doubts with people. And when you hear it, beware, because it's hard to trust a person who has to say "trust me." Why? If they must extol their own virtues, they're trying much too hard to convince you. Highly credible people don't need to do that; they just speak the factual truth. People who resort to "trust me, I know for a fact" are generally not trustworthy.

Remember the dictionary definition of the word "fact": "Something that has actual existence."[2] Everything else is not definitively a fact.

People randomly use these words to seal the deal, or argument, or sell the point they're trying to make. But their supposed "facts" are merely emphatic opinions.

So, here's what to do when somebody says, "Trust me, I know for a fact."

Ask them to support it with a real-life example or illustration.

If they can't come up with an example, be wary of what they're saying. If they do have factual, relevant examples, they're probably telling the truth, and not just selling or pitching something.

Chips Factorion is extremely confident about what he says, does, recommends, proposes, solves, and creates. Never once does he say, "Trust me, I know for a fact." He doesn't have to, and he wouldn't ever resort to that language.

He never says anything with the least bit of fluff because it's not at all in his mindset. But when he receives fluff from another person, watch out. He not only ignores or challenges it, but also turns completely off to the person and won't deal with them at all.

Mr. Factorion deals in facts, data, evidence, real versus contrived or assumed information, and plenty of factual examples to support his beliefs and arguments that convince people he's correct. And he usually is. His booming communications company, one of the America's fastest-growing firms in that space, supports that fact.

He welcomes one's opinion, and listens. But don't throw a bunch of off-the-wall opinions or unsubstantiated facts at him, because he'll nail you and probably not deal with you again. I've seen it happen on several occasions, and he's not alone. There are many other people in this world who are completely repulsed and turned off by ridiculous, act-less claims.

I've done business with the leader of a world-renowned healthcare company for several decades, and never once have I heard him say, "I know for a fact," or "Trust me." He doesn't have to.

Alda Cocker, on the other hand, is just the opposite. The old fart, as he calls himself, spouts off his mouth day in and day out, telling people how much he knows, and how smart he is. He says, "Trust me, I know for a fact" probably twenty-five times a day (who's counting?) . . . and trust me, nobody's really listening!

If those words are in your vocabulary, get rid of them today.

APPLYING THIS TO REAL LIFE

It's very simple. The moment you hear a person say, "I know for a fact," or even worse, "Trust me, I know for a fact," be very careful with what they're about to tell you.

If they speak in terms of facts and truisms, not unfounded opinions and exaggerations, they don't need to tell you they know for a fact. Or "trust me."

That usually means that much of what they say in their lives isn't very factual and truthful. Or, giving them the benefit of the doubt, it isn't always totally accurate . . . or it's simply stretched or put out of proportion.

Sadly, millions of people speak that way including people in major offices with lots of power.

My doctor father never ever used that language, and patients swore by him.

Don't ever catch yourself saying it. People will start to doubt you.

FLAXSEED FACTORS TO REMEMBER

1. When you hear somebody say, "I know for a fact," watch out!

2. Ask for examples, supportive data, or evidence. If they don't respond to that, beware.

3. Analyze what they're saying and separate fact from opinion, conclusion from inference.

4. The words "trust me" are a red flag. The speaker probably can't be believed or wouldn't use the words "trust me" to strengthen their cause.

5. Catch yourself the moment you're about to say these words. Think before you speak.

6. Credible, knowledgeable, confident people don't need to use those words. They never say "I know for a fact" . . . because they're loaded with facts and proven data . . . and people trust them.

7. Having to resort to this type of language diminishes credibility.

Five

Lesson to Unlearn #5

Trust People When They Say, "It's Confidential. I Give You My Word!"

Forget that!

How many times have you heard a person say that to you at work or in everyday conversation.

"I give you my word! I promise I won't tell a soul! Not one person!"

And in a matter of days, it's all around the office, the neighborhood, the universe . . . everywhere.

Some people, of course, do treat the word "confidential" as law. They stick to it 100 percent. Others say it but forgot they said it a day or two later.

Unfortunately, the word "confidential" can mean "maybe confidential" or "maybe not confidential." The word "confidential" is a handy, contrived word that is frequently misused and abused.

Even some lawyers, doctors, relatives, dear friends,

professionals like shrinks, therapists, and counselors can misuse and abuse it.

In fact, I remember a psychologist I bumped into at a social function once telling me, “Roger, don’t tell another person . . . but a patient I’m treating whom you and I know well went berserk the other day, is absolutely crazy, and is the biggest head case I’ve ever treated.” He told me to keep this confidential, and then subsequently told me who the person was. Hmmm! Completely unprofessional!

What some people assure you will be kept confidential will not necessarily be kept confidential. Especially in the business world . . . often identified as “gossip city.”

This is a tough chapter to write, but it’s important and very relevant.

It deals with one of the great lessons: People sworn to secrecy and confidentiality will not keep your secrets.

It’s serious stuff, a very sensitive topic, because it deals with somebody’s integrity, or the lack thereof.

Truism: When somebody tells you that you can count on them a hundred percent to keep to themselves what you told them, you’ve got a fifty-fifty chance they will. Sad but true. It’s human nature to talk too much. People will always be people!

It’s almost like when a person tells you . . . I’m 99.9 percent sure of something! That usually means they’re fifty-fifty certain, at best. Sounds cynical, I know, but some people often don't mean what they say.

The "100 percent confidentiality assurance" might actually mean . . . I will keep this 100 percent confidential, or perhaps 50 percent confidential . . . or not confidential at all, depending upon whom I'm speaking with.

Every day people will say that they'll keep something totally confidential, between "you and me," and what you tell them will not be shared with anybody, not a soul. So, you share something important and relevant with them that cannot go public.

And what do they sometimes do?

They let it out of the bag with another person, and say, for example . . .

"Give me your word that what I'm about to tell you will be kept 100 percent confidential, and you won't tell a soul. I assured Jo Ann Hurtz that I would keep what she told me totally confidential, but I must, nevertheless, share it with you."

And then they proceed to completely breach the verbal confidentiality agreement.

This lack of integrity and good, sound business ethics is deplorable. I don't want to come across preachy, didactic, holier than thou, or pedantic, but often what we learn "confidentially" is all over the place.

What I'm saying is that when somebody swears to

you that what you tell them will remain totally confidential, there's a good chance that will not be the case. They might tell other folks on the sly about a confidential thing they just heard and then get them to swear they won't share that information with anybody.

And what does that person do? They, in turn, share it with another person, requesting their confidentiality . . . and by the time the tenth person hears it, nobody even hears the words "confidential" anymore. Your confidential piece of information officially has become gossip, and we know how much many people love to gossip.

FYI, the word "confidential" is defined by *Merriam-Webster's Collegiate Dictionary* as . . .

"Intended for or restricted to the use of a particular person, group, or class."[3]

And the definition of "secret" is . . .

"Kept from knowledge or view."[4]

Aside from vital things like murder, kidnapping, treason, manslaughter, child abuse, or other serious things that could result in great harm and/or loss of life, confidentiality is like an ethical contract that must be abided by.

Another mistruth that's close to the definition of confidentiality, with a slightly different spin, is the legal term nondisclosure agreement, or frequently called an NDA.

An NDA is an agreement in which a person agrees to keep information such as a trade secret, new idea, potential innovation, etc. completely confidential.

It's purportedly a legally binding contract that establishes a confidential relationship. People who sign this NDA, or confidentiality agreement, acknowledge that there is extremely sensitive information they'll be receiving which cannot be made accessible to any other people, firms, organizations, etc.

OK. That sounds realistic and credible.

But even though sensitive information is being shared, you must be careful that the party receiving it will uphold this agreement. And it's difficult to find out if they do.

NDAs come in two forms: Mutual (both parties agree to be confidential), and nonmutual (one party agrees). Although an NDA is a legally binding agreement, and violating it can potentially lead to legal penalties, it still can be a very tenuous agreement that can or cannot be effectuated.

Enough said—I'm not a lawyer. But the area of "confidentiality" and how it is always upheld is clearly a lesson to unlearn.

A human resource acquaintance of mine often told me things that were confidentially told to him by fellow colleagues. He told me not to dare share the information with anybody.

One time, he told me about an employee who had "confided" in him that she was interviewing with another company and was uncertain whether to consider this new position.

So, what did the HR person do? He not only told me this confidential information, but he told the person's boss to "keep this confidential, but Wanda Jobs was considering resigning and going to another company."

As soon as Wanda's boss heard that, the ballgame was over. She later gave Wanda the silent treatment, ignored her when they passed each other in the hallway, and removed her from a key project.

Oh! Wanda decided to remain at the company and not take the other position, but she was a lame duck in the eyes of her boss, and her career spiraled downward.

Another ugly example of how this word is frequently violated occurred with an attorney. He mentioned that one of his clients was in financial trouble and his firm was considering going bankrupt. That was confidential information, but the lawyer told me that the firm was in financial trouble, and I wonder how many other people he told?

And finally, a major healthcare executive told his assistant to keep it quiet, but he was going in for major surgery. He didn't want the word out, however, for fear that much of his work would be taken away from him and given to other associates. The assistant "confidentially" told another person that the executive was going in for major surgery but asked him not to tell anybody. Of course, he told others, but "confidentially."

I rest my case about this lesson to unlearn! Don't take the word "confidential" as if it's a guaranteed fact. Forget that!

APPLYING THIS TO REAL LIFE

A few things to keep in mind regarding this lesson unlearned.

1. Avoid telling people anything they truly don't need to hear, especially if it borders on being confidential. Remember the "less is more" principle—often saying less is more effective.

2. If you must share some critical information with another person, and you want it kept confidential, first look them in the eye and say, "What I am about to tell you is 100 percent confidential,

and you must promise not to share this with anybody." Pause for a few seconds, look them in the eyes, and wait until they assure you that they will not divulge anything regarding what you are telling them.

Note that even when you hear that they won't divulge a thing, you never totally know if it will be held strictly confidential. But, of course, there are some people whom you can completely trust to be confidential, and I hope you know who they are.

3. In some cases, it might make sense to have the person sign a document that states they have heard confidential information and will not share it with anybody. This is better than nothing, but again, keep in mind that people tend to talk too much, and intentionally or unintentionally breach confidentiality.

4. If you, personally, are told something in total confidentiality, consider that a contract and never breach it.

In short, be very careful when you hear the words "I swear I won't tell anybody what you told me . . . I give you my word." It may come back to haunt you.

If it is not totally necessary to tell someone something that borders on being confidential, take a deep breath and consider whether you want to tell them this information.

A day later, you might be very happy you said nothing. You realize that you didn't really need to say anything, anyway, as is the case in many instances in life. Less is more.

Remember the potential cons of confidentiality and NDAs—the whole subject of confidentiality can create an atmosphere of mistrust and can sour relationships with other colleagues. It can even make people paranoid. Who needs that?

FLAXSEED FACTORS TO REMEMBER

1. When somebody asks you to keep something confidential, consider that request as a contract. Don't violate it. The only time you should consider breaching the confidentiality is if the subject of life or death, or serious harm is involved, or "legal or illegal" is the issue.

2. Don't take what you just read as the end-all fact. I am an author, not a lawyer. Either consult with a lawyer about this matter, or at least confer with a senior executive and/or HR professional in your organization to get their advice and counsel.

3. When you ask somebody to keep something totally confidential, realize what might occur. That is, it is sometimes not kept totally confidential.

4. Nondisclosure agreements (NDAs) are legal documents. Consider seeing an attorney before you get involved in one.

Part Two

Things We Learned in Grade School

"We've got to beat Peebsland High School in baseball. They're our biggest rivalry. If we lose to them, the season's a bust. Winning is everything!"

"Adults are infallible, and we should listen to and follow all that they say. Ditto schoolteachers who share important life lessons with us every day."

These are just two examples of things we learned in grade school that are incorrect.

As a child, it's totally normal to believe that all you're learning at school and at home from parents is correct. But as we grow up and experience real-life incidents, we see that many of those things learned in grade school and at home were not in our best interests. Or they were in our best interests, but wrong!

For example, many of us were told things like

"Being cold gets you sick," or "Breakfast is the most important meal of the day," or "Christopher Columbus discovered North America." All of these are myths that have permeated through generations.

Adults are indeed fallible—they make mistakes. And they go through life making the same mistakes repeatedly.

But the older we get, the more we come to realize that adults, in general, make their share of mistakes. That includes our parents and teachers.

This section covers several of those life lessons that need to be unlearned immediately. You'll see why when you go through them.

Six

Lesson to Unlearn #6

Winning Is Everything; Losing Stinks

One of pro football's most successful and well-known coaches of all time, Vince Lombardi, created the famous quote, "Winning isn't everything; it's the only thing."

It quickly spread across the country and has been around for decades. Coaches in all sports often quote it. They even place large signs in the locker rooms to remind their players. Later in life, Lombardi said that what he meant was "the will to win" or "making an effort." But the original quote stuck in the minds of millions.

How unrealistic and detrimental is that thought? It's a dangerous myth that creates bad behaviors and actions and can lead to shattered dreams! Forget that!

Losing can be a wonderful game-changer.

One of the life-changing things about losing is that it often teaches you how to be better. How to grow, develop, and gain such value from the loss that you have a chance at winning the next time, or in the future. It gives you the impetus to try to do better.

The quote "Winning isn't everything; it's the only thing" elicits two diametrically opposed reactions in countless people.

On the one hand . . . it inspires people to try hard. Makes winning and doing your best, not only in sports, but in life, an important mindset, and drives people to set high goals for themselves. And many people use that quote to motivate themselves. That's the good news.

On the other hand, it has misled, even devastated, the morale and spirit of millions of people. It has made thousands of people crazed and totally consumed with winning, at almost any cost.

It's a very damaging thought.

Why? Because there is only one winner, whether it's a game, a job position, a deal . . . you name it . . . the other person, side, or team simply cannot win.

And because people are obsessed with winning, they sometimes never get over the fact that they lost.

Also, parents of young kids who play a sport just to have fun, who are obsessed with the child winning, take the fun out of the game for the kid.

But as world-renowned, legendary golfer Arnold Palmer once declared, "Winning isn't everything, but wanting it is."

A person often learns more from losing than from winning. You learn how to keep going. Sure, people hate losing, often feeling that they're not as good as they had thought, and even feel somewhat out of control.

But think of the benefits of losing. One of the most valuable things a person can learn in life is how to deal with the emotions and pain of losing. Winning everything, which almost never happens, curbs your ability to cope with losses and stressful experiences.

Losing with dignity builds character and makes you a better human being. Losses shape weaknesses and shortcomings, and make you focus on improvement, growth, and winning the next time. If you learn from a loss, you haven't really lost at all.

I remember vividly a college tennis match I had against nationally ranked and three-time Atlantic Coast Conference tennis player George Sokol of the University of North Carolina. I faced him in the quarter finals of the Atlantic Coast Conference (ACC) tennis championships, and he had just played a close match with Rafael Osuna, who was ranked top five in the world and had won the US Open and Wimbledon doubles championships.

I thought I had zero chance of upsetting Sokol,

but shockingly, I pulled out to a 4-1 first-set lead. I remember it was around ninety-five degrees that humid North Carolina day, and I was totally exhausted from putting everything I had into those first five games. Meanwhile, Sokol was just taking off his warm-up sweat suit. I couldn't move, and he was just warming up. How depressing!

I lost my focus, thought about this potential big upset, was fully exhausted, while Sokol was apparently just getting started. As I daydreamed about how exciting this potential upset would be, he proceeded to win the next eleven straight games in around twenty-five minutes. After losing the first set, and dropping the first three games of the second, I quickly became discouraged and mentally gave up.

I was emotionally devastated but Coach Doyle Royal (yeah, that's what his name was) sat me down afterward and gave me five life lessons from the loss:

There's always something to be gained from a loss, a "take-home" . . . Never ever lose focus . . . Pace yourself in everything you do . . . Don't ever rest on your past laurels . . . and never ever give up, even if there's "nothing left in the gas tank."

Five valuable lessons I've taken with me to the business and parenting world and would never have learned without that losing experience. In hindsight, I actually won that day. Well, kind of.

That might be an example in competitive sports, but it's the exact same in the real world.

Let's also periodically substitute the word "winning" with the word "win-winning." That's where both sides feel they've won, even if a little.

At times, winning might be impossible, but both sides winning, "win-winning," is a mutual victory. In the George Sokol tennis contest, he won the match, but I won some life lessons. A win-win.

Stuart Allendale was at the top of his game in human resources. He was the chief learning officer of a leading company, on his way to becoming its top HR person globally. Shockingly, he didn't get it. And worse, he was told that his energy was not there as it used to be.

So, for whatever reason, Stuart left the company bewildered and down. He felt like he had lost, because getting the top HR position globally would represent a huge win for him. And that depressed him . . . well, for only a while. But he actually had won. No longer beholden to the company, he went on to become vice chairman of a major healthcare organization and build a thriving consulting business. A great example of "winning is not all that matters . . . and if you lose, you can come right back and be a winner!"

Nelson Mandela, former president of South Africa, put it succinctly: "I never lose. I either win or I learn."

And Ultimate Fighter celebrity "Irish Joe" Duffy, UFC mixed martial artist, said it all upon retiring: "Losing isn't always the end. Sometimes it's the beginning."

APPLYING THIS TO REAL LIFE

Of course, everybody in the world wants to win. That's human nature. Find me a person who says they didn't want to win, and you'll find me a liar.

Winning feels good for all of us. But losing is not that bad also. From losing, we learn perhaps how to win the next time, or how to be better, in general.

It's normal to be down, out, discouraged, even depressed a bit from losing something you wanted to win badly, or feel like you should have won.

But after a while, try to dismiss the emotion and hurt of losing, and turn it into an opportunity to really gain something . . . to grow . . . to end up winning something. This could even be much greater than the victory one feels when winning. Much greater, indeed.

Adopt this as a way of life. Nobody in the world, nobody, wins everything. But losing can, in the long run, be much better than winning, or that wonderful experience you felt after you won.

How do you adopt this important life lesson about winning?

1. Wanting to win badly makes you the winner. If you've tried very hard, but lost, you've won because you put in a great effort. And in the long run, great effort leads to great results.

2. Try to do your very best in everything you do. That attitude will rub off on everything you do in life. The antithesis of that attitude will also run off on everything you do, but negatively.

3. "Shoot for the moon," a Les Brown quote says. "Even if you don't land there, you'll reach the stars."[5]

4. Remind yourself that in every contest or competition, somebody's got to win, and somebody's got to lose. That's life.

5. Be obsessed with trying to win but realize that #4 (above) is a fact of life. Only one winner, but that doesn't mean you can't be totally driven to be that person.

6. Gain from your losses. There's always something to learn from coming in second, third, or last. Not pondering what that "something" is represents a lost opportunity for you.

7. Winning isn't always getting ahead of others. It also means getting ahead of yourself, improving, growing, developing further.

8. Stay positive. Don't let negativity enter your mind. If it does, or if a person spouts negativity, dispel it or go far away from it. It's toxic and energy-debilitating.

FLAXSEED FACTORS TO REMEMBER

1. Winning is overrated and overemphasized, and sometimes causes individuals to get out of control. It can be traumatic.

2. Losing, when growing and benefiting from it, is a win.

3. When you analyze why you have lost, you have potentially gained more than the person who has won, who might become complacent.

4. Winning doesn't always mean you won the game and came in first. Or won the deal and will reap the benefits! It can also mean that you've done better than you ever have before. You've improved, developed, grown! And the more you lose, the more you want to win in the future.

5. Turn a painful negative into a life-changing positive.

6. Winning isn't everything, but wanting to win is.

Seven

Lesson to Unlearn #7

Those with the Highest Grades Become the Most Successful

What do these seventeen enormously successful people have in common?

Walt Disney (Disney)
Paul Allen (Microsoft cofounder)
Larry Ellison (Oracle)
Tom Cruise (Actor)
Mark Zuckerberg (Facebook)
Lady Gaga (Recording artist/performer)
James Cameron (*Titanic*, *Avatar*, *Aliens*)
Ralph Lauren (Polo, Ralph Lauren)
Frank Lloyd Wright (Architect/Guggenheim Museum)
Jay-Z (Rapper)
Evan Williams (Twitter)

Jawed Karim (YouTube)
Richard Branson (Virgin Group)
Jack Dorsey (Twitter)
Steve Jobs (Apple)
Elton John (Singer/entertainer)
Bill Gates (Microsoft cofounder)

These individuals, some of the world's most successful people ever, dropped out of school. Can you believe that?

So here we go again. A myth and unsubstantiated thought that was created generations ago is simply not true. And growing up, how many times did we hear "You've got to get your education to be successful." Forget that!

I love author and radio host Tom Bodett's quote:

"The difference between school and life? In school, you're taught a lesson and given a test. In life, you're given a test that teaches you a lesson."

Brilliant quote, Tom, and so true. Thanks. And when I look at the list above, I see what you mean.

Sure, the A student in school has a great chance of becoming the A player in the field they go in, assuming they possess the right attitude, interpersonal skills, and motivation to succeed.

But being an A student, or ranking high in your class, doesn't guarantee you anything. Zero. Nada.

And being a PhD graduate from Harvard, or an

MBA from Stanford or Columbia, surely doesn't hurt you. But does it assure you anything?

Nope!

Street smarts, common sense, and risk-taking can take you very far in life. Even to the top. Those people mentioned above are some of the most successful people you'll ever hear of.

There are A students who might be rocket scientists and academic geniuses but who have struggled in their careers for decades, still searching for that home run in life. But some of these A students get a D minus in interpersonal skills or creativity.

Alton Gascon was a straight-A student in high school and college, and near the top of his medical school class.

He had his own medical practice, did okay, but never exceptionally well, especially for a gifted physician. The reason: He was known as a know-it-all, bragging, overly talkative, hugely opinionated, poor listener who constantly interrupted others. And in a subtle way, he let everybody know how intelligent he was.

Alton still wonders why he just didn't do that well as a physician. The answer is obvious, and wonderful grades in school turned out to be a nonissue in his career. Nobody asked about them nor cared.

And then, there are people like a kid I knew in college, Sacha Paine, who absolutely hated school, got awful grades, and barely made it through. But he landed a position on the ground floor with one of the world's most successful technology startups ever.

Sacha apparently made hundreds of millions of dollars and certainly not because he was a model student in the classroom. But he was a genius in street-smart, commonsense intelligence, communicating effectively and winning people over with decisiveness, problem-solving, and emotional intelligence. And he had energy that went through the roof!

AN AMAZING, WONDERFUL STORY

Bob Fivis, a self-made mega success story, who graduated high school at age fifteen, went right to work because he and his family had very little money. He never even attended college because he couldn't afford it.

Subsequently, Bob met a guy named Chuck who started a discount-brokerage financial firm in the seventies. Chuck asked street-smart Bob to help him out in the finance area, as his small, unknown company began to grow. Bob never had a finance course in his life, but he sure was credible and likable. Plus, he was a quick study and a sponge for learning.

Over the years, Chuck built up his company to one of the world's most respected bank and stock brokerage firms, as Bob became his go-to chief financial officer.

Kudos to Bob Fivis for grinding it out and reaching financial stardom . . . and kudos to Chuck who had the intuition to broker stocks at hugely discounted commission rates. And to hire Mr. Fivis.

Oh, Chuck also went by the name Charles, and his firm, the Charles Schwab Corporation, is still a giant in the industry.

Quite a story, huh!

And quite an example of how the best grades don't always produce the best success. Plus, going to college is fine, but guarantees nothing.

Me? I got lots of B's, a few A's, and my share of C's. And I remember failing an anthropology course because I loathed the subject. When I did, I asked myself why I was going to college.

I was nowhere near a top student at all. In my family of five, I'm number five on the list of brain power. But common sense, some street smarts, and an insatiable passion to make something of myself has driven me much further than any A grade would have taken me. And helped me get a PhD degree. Incidentally, that PhD degree might have been enriching, but it taught me nothing about life. I learned that lesson when I went out to the real world. I'm clearly not a rocket scientist. And nowhere near those people listed above. But who cares?

APPLYING THIS TO REAL LIFE

Enough of the myth that book-smart people are the ones that go the furthest.

Or the mistruth that you've got to get great grades and attend college to go places in life.

Excellent grades certainly can help you. But they're not a guarantee that you're going to be successful at work, regardless of what you do in your career. They are simply scores on how well you know the subject matter your teachers have assigned you. They have little or nothing to do with the real world, although in some occupations and professions, they do mean more than other fields.

But top grades don't make you a top people person. Or a top innovator. Or an inspiring, results-oriented person. Or simply a winner.

They are only a piece of the puzzle of making it. It's a mistruth that has hindered millions of kids and adults, everywhere, and even usurped a great deal of their confidence, passion, and drive to succeed.

Others have gotten poor grades and proved to the world how talented and intelligent they were. And some didn't even go past high school, but they accomplished huge things in their lives.

Work hard to get the best grades possible, especially in areas that meaningfully apply to what you want to do in your life.

But if, for whatever reason, your grades don't cut it, just work harder, better, and more creatively, with tons of energy, enthusiasm, and passion. Those three traits come from loving what you do.

So, what's the sub-lesson learned? Try doing what you love to do, have great interest in, and feel like you can be successful in. Don't let the lack of huge academic success deter or discourage you.

This goes for people of all ages, who dream of accomplishing something big, but aren't sure they can accomplish it. It's never too late to start.

It's all a state of mind, not a state of intellect or brilliance. If you're in the middle of a career and go back to school, cool. But let what you gain from past learning experiences drive you, not just the thirst for getting all A's in your courses.

The key: To be successful in anything you do, you must have your heart completely embedded in your work—your business idea, dream, work ethic, everything.

Your heart is where you work from, and it's the foundation of success. It drives you in your business, and rubs off on colleagues, customers, and collaborators. It can be infectious to others and inspiring to customers and prospects, as well as your team. Heart-driven people motivate other people. And they learn to emulate you, which is Motivation 101.

It's easy to spot a driven heart in a person. That is the fuel that lights up your fire each and every day.

FLAXSEED FACTORS TO REMEMBER

1. Good grades, studying hard, and grinding it out will never hurt you.

2. But nothing succeeds like street-smart, common-sense thinking and executing excellent people skills, learning from your mistakes, and optimizing good opportunities and timing.

3. You don't need to be a rocket scientist to learn about and identify problems, discover needs, invent something, or establish strategies and game plans that meet those needs. Lots of it is simply common sense.

4. Thinking that the top students become the most successful people is preposterous. Many wonderful students failed to become successful later in life.

5. You don't need A's in school, high grades, or even a college degree to become a great communicator, a

spot-on problem solver, a strong relationship builder, an ongoing inspirer, and a decisive, take-charge leader. Look at Walt Disney, Larry Ellison, Lady Gaga, and Bill Gates, among many others.

6. As American writer, futurist, and businessperson Alvin Toffler stated: "Tomorrow's illiterate will not be the man who can't read; he will be the man who has not learned how to learn."[6] It clearly doesn't take great grades to be a great learner. That says it all!

Eight
Lesson to Unlearn #8
Wake Up and Stop Dreaming So Much

How many times have we been told to stop dreaming so much? Or to deal with reality and not some far-out dream that can't come true?

I heard that request many times when growing up and even when entering the business world. In fact, I still hear it once in a while. Forget that!

Dreams are healthy and can come true. But they do so when we proactively make them happen, if that's doable. They don't necessarily become reality just because we dreamed them up and wished they'd come true.

Don't get me wrong. I don't want to sound like a pessimist or skeptic. That's the exact opposite of who I am. My glass is half filled, not half empty; I'm usually excited about potential new ideas, brainstorming, and innovation.

As a youngster, I was often called the "cockeyed

optimist." I dreamed and envisioned ideas all the time, regardless of their soundness or research done on the idea. Today, I'm still dreaming because it's an upbeat feeling, fun, and probably healthy for the heart.

But the fact is, constantly dreaming of things that never come true can quickly get old and depressing. There's a thin line between healthy and unhealthy dreaming.

First rule: You must be a realist who sees through the BS (and the BS artists) quickly.

Try to disassociate yourself from people who dream big, but with no real thought, logic, or sense of reality. Be a pragmatist who separates fact from opinion, hype from reality, wild, unreachable dreams from truly interesting opportunities. Look for the sound theory and rationale associated with the dream, and its potential application.

If you dream of something happening, and it finally comes true, kudos and congrats to you. That's wonderful.

But I see so many people who are what I call "psychotic dreamers." People who dream of things that have absolutely no way of coming true, and they do little or nothing to actualize these dreams. So, they live a life of frustration and disappointment. Many of them are very angry that things never worked out the way they dreamed they would.

Neal Charlotsky set his dreams on being a self-made businessperson, successful enough to enjoy the good life and have a family at a relatively early age. He dreamed of a beautiful home in the suburbs, a vacation home in the Berkshires, and lots of time with friends, family, and his dog.

But he did more than dream. He set up a strategy and game plan to do everything possible to see those dreams become reality. He worked like a dog, 24-7, to make that dream come true, and it did. He built his company up so much that it was acquired by a public company.

Dick Dickerson dreamed of being an award-winning film producer, entrepreneur, businessperson, deal maker, and owner of homes on both coasts. Yes, he dreamed of these things, but none came true because all he did was dream. He had no sustained follow-through. Over thirty years after he started his career, he was still dreaming big, talking big, but actualizing nothing. A very sad, depressing example of a "psychotic dreamer."

I dreamed all my life of starting a company that would be on the New York Stock Exchange. Big dreams but fun to wish for. And I also dreamed of writing a movie and watching it on TV with my family and friends.

I had those dreams since high school and did everything possible to make them come true. And thankfully, both did, and that satisfaction continues to inspire me as the years pass.

My training/consulting firm ended up being acquired by a NY Stock Exchange company, and my film, *The Last Home Run* ended up playing on HBO and Showtime.

And yes, I watched it on TV one Saturday afternoon with my family, three sons, and their friends. In that film, I created the expression "If you stop dreaming, you stop living," and that's been my mantra ever since.

I have a buddy, Vaughn "Bake" Baker, whom I played with on the University of Maryland tennis team. He recently told me that he fell in love with pickleball and plays it all the time.

He also told me that someday, he dreams of being a national pickleball champion. Even in the senior player's bracket. Bake is still dreaming like a kid!

And a guy I've known for many years retired and moved to Florida. So, what's on his mind? He bought a beautiful condominium and dreams of being the president of the condo association someday. Sounds like a headache to me, especially with the devastating hurricanes that have happened there, but at least it's his dream.

Don't get me wrong, I believe in dreaming, and dreaming big . . . and so should you. But be realistic with your dreams, and how you can possibly make them come true.

APPLYING THIS TO REAL LIFE

Yes, dreams do come true, but not automatically. Dreams come true when they are sensible and actionable.

Here's a twelve-step process for creating dreams, analyzing whether they are sensible, managing them, and doing everything possible to make them come true.

1. **Face the facts.** Realize that it's wonderful to dream, so go ahead and dream all you want. Some of the world's most successful people, like Walt Disney, Bill Gates, Steve Jobs, and Warren Buffet dreamed big and constantly thought of ways to make their dreams and visions become reality.

   Daydream when you're running, walking, swimming (if you do), sitting around, traveling on an airplane, on a long trip, whenever you're in the mood. Keep thinking of what that wonderful dream is, but don't just stop there. **For that dream to become a reality, you must commit to making it happen.** Face that fact now, or at least carefully ponder it. If you face that fact, you'll save yourself a lot of time in the short and long run. And you'll reduce disappointment and frustration.

2. **Be honest with yourself.** Analyze the dream in terms of real-life application. In short, is it feasible

and achievable and something that you'll commit to following up on?

3. **Define the realistic outcome you would like to attain from the dream.** What exactly is that hypothetical outcome, what does it look and sound like, what do you want to see happen because of working diligently to try making the dream come true?

4. **Establish goals, subgoals, and relevant timeframes** to work on to turn the dream into reality. Be firm and disciplined with yourself to follow through.

5. **Be honest with yourself and get real.** Is there a need that exists in this world for what you're dreaming of? Is it worth going after? And if it's a personal dream, is it sensible, or so far-out that there's no way it'll come true?

6. **If it is worth pursuing, define your follow-up action plans.**
    a. What do you specifically need to do?
    b. What is your game plan?
    c. Who, if anyone, do you need to collaborate with?

   d. What are the specific next steps you must take to actualize the dream?
   e. What are the measurables and check points that will tell you if you're making progress?

7. **Determine what the obstacles are now or might be in the future.** What are the roadblocks and challenges to attaining the dream? Ask yourself if all of this is worth your time.

8. **Re-evaluate your timeframes and time parameters** for the work that needs to be done to accomplish the dream and make it successful.

9. **Be fully committed to spending the necessary time** to make the dream come true. Be your own devil's advocate to ensure this is what you want to do.

10. **Go after the dream with a vengeance.** Make it part of your life. Let the dream drive you and give you a purpose. And when the dream does come true, reward yourself, celebrate, enjoy your results.

11. **Start to redream.** Start thinking of another goal that would be fun to go after and develop. Go through the same steps as above.

12. **Remember**, when you stop dreaming, you stop living. You are never too old to dream.

Hard work pays huge dividends. Dreams become goals . . . goals become actions . . . actions require hard work and overcoming obstacles . . . risk is part of the equation . . . but dreams do come true.

If you happen to dream of something that could be an exciting part of your life, and it does finally come true, kudos and congrats. That's wonderful. Reward yourself.

And don't let anybody tell you that you dream too much.

"When you stop dreaming, you stop living."

FLAXSEED FACTORS TO REMEMBER

1. Dreaming is one of our great gifts. It's good to dream of things . . . but important to dream realistically.

2. No dream is too far-out, as long it is attainable and not an out-of-sight hope that's impossible to achieve.

3. Use a formal approach to your dreams. Go through the twelve-step process, check off the boxes, and see if that dream might work for you.

4. Remember: If you stop dreaming, you stop living. We all need to have dreams, big, small, or in between. Dreaming has been part of our lives since childhood and should never end.

5. Don't accept people saying that you dream too much. But avoid being a "psychotic dreamer" whose dreams are just unattainable delusions.

Nine
Lesson to Unlearn #9
Don't Speak to Strangers

I was sitting on a plane recently and takeoff was delayed.

I didn't have much to do except wonder if we'd ever take off and how long the delay would be.

So, I began a conversation with the woman sitting next to me. There was not much else to do except read the airline's magazine or close my eyes.

Before I knew it, the conversation livened, and a mutual business interest between us was discovered.

She ran a foundation and asked what I did for a living. After I told her, she said she was interested in her colleagues going through my "High-Impact Presentations" training and coaching program.

Yes, most of these airplane sitting-next-to-another-person conversations lead to nowhere.

But this one had legs. She took my card, called me

in a week, set up a meeting, and decided to contract my firm for training and coaching services.

She's now a client of mine, and we've contracted for a series of programs. And she plans to offer our program to her clients, who are major municipality and county and state government groups. The number of business opportunities seems unlimited.

All because of speaking to a stranger.

I can list a bunch of other examples of speaking to strangers and where it led, including speaking to a woman whom I had never met before, hiring her for my company, and ultimately being introduced to her best friend.

Oh! That best friend of hers is my wife of many years.

I was riding my bike on Strickland Avenue in Chadwick Beach, NJ. I saw a guy serving tennis balls by himself, pounding the ball at least 107.33 miles per hour. The guy looked like a good player; at least, he clearly had a great serve. And I liked his hat.

So, I pulled over to the fence and complimented him on his serve and asked if he'd like to play one of these days. He agreed to and then in our brief conversation asked me what I did for a living, and I asked the same of him.

When he heard I was in the leadership development

consulting business, he asked me if I had ever written a book. I told him I was in the process of completing one.

When I asked him what he did for a living, he told me he was the publisher and head of audiobooks for one of the world's largest book publishing companies, Hachette Book Group.

Hmm! My lightbulb went on and shined all around Strickland Avenue.

He asked me if he could read my book and of course I said, "Sure." Next thing I know is that he called me to tell me he'd like to publish the book.

The rest is history. My first book, *No Stopping You! How to Win the Game of Life* is the book that he and Hachette published, and *Forget That! 22 Lessons You Must Unlearn to Succeed* is the second book of mine he's published, with Blackstone Publishing, his new employer. All started by talking to a stranger one hot summer day in July.

NOBODY SAID IT WAS EASY

For many people, the thought of starting a conversation with a complete stranger is nerve-racking at best and completely stressful at worst. I'm not at all suggesting you go up to every Tom, Dick, or Harriet and start a conversation with them.

I'm suggesting that you get out of the habit of not talking to strangers, and at least have an open mind about initiating conversations with strangers, or people whom you hardly know. That is . . . if it is appropriate, natural, and comfortable to do, and you're not pushing yourself in their face.

The world is full of so many interesting, diversified, connected people. And so many unbelievable opportunities that you might never hear about. And who knows what could happen if you connect with a person whom otherwise you would never utter a word to.

The truth is . . . you have nothing to lose with widening your network of contacts, future friends, or future business associates. The fun is in the chase, even with relationship building.

If I never had said hello to the woman sitting next to me on the flight, nothing would have resulted.

New lesson learned: The next time the opportunity and timing are right, engage or at least say hello to that person you just saw, and whom you might have something in common with. Don't get in their face and be pushy or aggressive. Just initiate a conversation.

There is no downside other than getting ignored, shrugged off, or smirked at. But who cares! The upside could be plentiful.

The worst-case scenario is that it goes nowhere. You spent a few minutes acquainting yourself with a new person.

The best-case scenario could be that you find a

commonality of interest, be it personal, professional, or whatever . . . and you take it to the next level.

People call this networking. I call it simply being a people person who looks to meet new people and build relationships.

The new part-time lifeguard where I swim each day came up to me, introduced himself, and quickly impressed me with his charisma and confidence. When he told me that lifeguarding was an in-between job for him . . . in between his recent college graduation and looking for a full-time position in sales or marketing, I suggested he contact me.

Now, we're discussing a position for him to sell and market my firm's consulting services.

Now don't go around stopping people and pushing yourself on them. That's not what I mean at all. But you never know when you meet a person whether there is common ground and something mutually beneficial ahead.

I find it exciting and interesting to meet new people. Put this behavior on your action list—meet at least one new person every week. Who knows where it might lead?

APPLYING THIS TO REAL LIFE

Initiating small talk, as awkward as it may seem, is not a bad way to start a relationship with a new person. It breaks the ice and often reveals commonalities between you and the other person.

Often, we hope that the other person will take the first step and initiate the conversation. But it usually doesn't happen that way, so you might have to be the one who does it.

Project positivity and be upbeat and enthusiastic. Most people are positively affected by enthusiastic people, and enthusiasm can set the groundwork for a potential relationship, or at least, the beginning of a conversation. If you've been socially uncomfortable with that in the past, it can pave the way to a new you and an improved way to network with people.

Perhaps ask for advice or ask a few relevant questions, based on where you are and what the circumstances are. It keeps the dialogue open and possibly leads to an area of the conversation that has mutual interest. If you hear something that sparks a side conversation, pursue it. Suddenly, you and the other person have something in common, and the rest starts to flow and be less uncomfortable.

Do more listening than talking, a rule stressed earlier in this book. When you show sincere interest by listening, and don't interrupt, the other person usually appreciates this and reciprocates the kind gesture. Plus, actively listening with good eye contact might give you nonverbal cues, which could also lead to something interesting or different.

Based on how the chemistry goes, and if it comes naturally, you might want to communicate how to follow up on this short conversation, especially if there is a commonality of chemistry. You can sense that commonality or not and decide on the next step.

I know this all might be foreign to you, but it also might open doors that normally would be closed to you. This book would not have a publisher if I hadn't spoken to a complete stranger on court number three.

FLAXSEED FACTORS TO REMEMBER

1. Not speaking with strangers should not be a rule set in stone. You never know where that initial communication could lead. It might be interesting and mutually beneficial, but you never know unless you try.

2. Be tactful, courteous, and nonpushy when initiating a conversation with a person you don't know. Don't come on strong or obtrusive.

3. Listen much more than you speak. As much as 80 percent of the dialogue should come from the other person. If you sense initial mutual interest, be more of a fact finder and concerned listener than a person who blatantly pushes to establish a relationship.

4. At the end of the conversation, pause for a moment to see if she or he wants to continue the relationship or specifically follow up on something. That tiny pause could (or could not) elicit a comment or action from the other person, and it is a good litmus test to see it it's worthwhile to pursue the next step.

5. Follow the five Ls: Be Laid back, Low-key, Light, Likable, and Listen. Never come on strong, especially at the get-go. Be warm, interesting, cordial. Don't be aggressive, overwhelming, or pushy.

6. If you are uncomfortable with speaking to strangers, and it's not your style at all, then consider scrapping this chapter. But don't throw in the towel too quickly. At least reread the examples presented above. They could happen with anybody. As I mentioned, the publishing of this book came from me speaking with a stranger. Now he's my "publisher for life," and a great buddy! (With a rocket tennis serve.) And he has a new, enjoyable Platform Tennis League he plays in all winter, the result of two strangers interacting.

Ten
Lesson to Unlearn #10
Save It for a Rainy Day

I must have heard my mom tell me this a gazillion times.

And my dad told me that his father didn't save his money well and when the depression came, he was all washed-up financially and lived the rest of his life in poverty. When my dad told me the story, it traumatized me. I still think about it frequently.

So many other people over the years have echoed this rainy-day sentiment. "Rainy day" is a metaphor for when a person experiences serious needs but is in financial straits and doesn't have the money to take care of their needs. A scary thought.

Apparently, this expression was born in the sixteenth century in Britain. According to BookBrowse, its first known use was in a play called *The Bugbears* in around 1561.

The words went like this . . .

"Wold he haue me kepe nothing against a raynye day?"

Translated into today's English, meaning . . .

"Would he have me keep nothing for a rainy day?"[7]

Sure, there's some twenty-first-century meaning in that logic created close to five centuries ago. Nobody would ever argue that it's not wise to save substantial money for the future, in case an emergency or serious need surfaces.

This makes sense to a great degree, of course, but it also can be a stymying factor that exerts a huge influence on the quality of your life. And not necessarily a positive one.

Inherent in the rationale behind this rainy-day theory is that you're saving money and putting something aside for a future time of sudden great need or extreme crisis.

That concern is legitimate, and everybody should follow that lesson and put away rainy-day money. After all, what's worse than the helpless, destitute feeling when you need money for an emergency and don't have it? You're strapped, and don't know where to turn. I can't imagine how helpless my grandfather must have felt when the depression led him to poverty.

Who knows if that will ever happen? Hopefully never, but poverty-stricken crises created by the recessions, or the COVID-19 pandemic, for example, caused rainy days for millions of people and small to medium-sized businesses all over the world. OK, I've painted enough negative pictures.

But here's the downside of this rainy-day mistruth.

Many people, due to this type of thinking, tend to live their lives with the sole intention of putting their nest egg away for only later in life . . . when they retire, get old, become ill, or desperately need it. Putting all or most of their hard-earned money aside until they critically need it.

The problem with that rationale is that some people forget to live their lives.

They forget to enjoy each day to the fullest, and to do plenty of fun and rewarding things with their hard-earned money. They're just too frugal.

Noah Spenderman had almost every dollar he had ever made. Did quite well over the years, but hadn't done anything with his life, other than work like a dog. His wife begged him to take time off and "get a life" before it was too late. He didn't want to spend the money to go out and splurge . . . take a cruise, rent a vacation home, or even do improvements on his home.

One day, some startling news hit Noah smack between the eyes. He was diagnosed with cancer. And tragically, he was told he didn't have much time to live.

Shocking and heartbreaking, but sadly, nothing could help him live longer, although docs tried everything.

He passed away quickly, never having spent money on anything because he saved it all for a rainy day.

Unfortunately, it more than rained.

I've got a colleague who makes a lot of money but won't spend a nickel on anything unless it is seriously needed. And that goes for his family—he won't do things that cost money because "it's just not worth what it costs."

Now he's up there in years and complains that all he did during his life was work and not "play." And his wife left him years ago; his kids are grown up and out of the house . . . and he has nobody to spend all that cash he's accumulated on.

Ditto my father, an obstetrician/gynecologist who worked seven days a week, even evenings, and never spent a dime on himself. However, he wasn't frugal with our family—we did fine—but he never did things to enjoy himself, because all he did was work and save.

Tragically, in the hospital bed after a major stroke, he confided in me, right before his death, that he regretted that he forgot to have any fun during his life. He said that he wished he could be a kid again. I took his sad remarks and built a feel-good movie around it, *The Last Home*

Run, that aired on HBO and Showtime. A story about an old doctor who's transformed into a twelve-year-old kid again, a Little League player, for five days.

We all save money with good intentions, but going overboard and putting away all or most of it can lead to huge regrets later.

You might wake up one day and suddenly feel depressed, as Noah and my dad did. You look back on the many years of your life when you should have been living it up and spending your money on enjoyable things. You can never replace that time.

My late mom wrote this little poem that I think about all the time . . .

"Enjoy each moment while you may . . . too soon it will be yesterday." Pretty telling thought, Mom!

The key thing with saving effectively is to ask yourself . . . "When do I stop saving everything and firmly draw the line?"

What if the rainy day, thankfully, doesn't come . . . or when it appears, you can't do anything about it, like what happened to Noah Spenderman and my dad?

What happens if you've been working tirelessly your entire life, day in and day out, and saving profusely for years, spending your money only on frightening emergencies, and not having much enjoyment?

If that's you, think deeply about this lesson to unlearn.

APPLYING THIS TO REAL LIFE

Save wisely, spend wisely. Don't throw your money away ruthlessly, and don't put it away endlessly.

Somewhere in the middle is the answer. Use the "why / why not" quick formula if it helps you decide:

Ask yourself, why should I spend that money, what is the reason, the benefit, the purpose, the enjoyment, etc.? Versus why not spend the money? What's the reason, the benefit, the purpose, the gain for not spending it on enjoyable things that bring you pleasure?

And then decide. This is especially wise advice for people who feel the pain every time they spend a dollar. If you're one of those people, perhaps remind yourself that life is short.

And remind yourself of the difference between the dictionary definitions of "frugal" and "cheapskate," "spendthrift" and "miser":

> **Frugal**—characterized by or reflecting economy in the use of resources.[8]
>
> **Cheapskate**—a miserly or stingy person[9]
>
> **Spendthrift**—a person who spends improvidently or wastefully[10]
>
> **Miser**—a mean grasping person[11]

Where do you stand?

IDEAS TO CONSIDER: Saving money with little or no effort.

Implementing a few of these ideas will put more money in your pocket, and bank account.

*Take a serious look at what you're spending on credit cards. The annual amount might make you nauseous. Negotiate credit card rates and even consider transferring what's owed to another credit card company.

*Make a commitment: Use credit cards 50 percent less from today on. Be disciplined. And if you don't have tax advantages from using credit cards, consider not using them at all.

*Take mental inventory of what your debt looks like. Pay it down as much as possible. Negotiate with the other party to see how that amount can be reduced or even forgiven, especially if you've been a good customer.

*Inquire as to what your benefits are costing you. Is there any way you can shave that down, or at least shop around for better, less expensive plans? They are out there.

*Have a financial planner / accountant help you assess what you need for a comfortable, stress-free retirement.

*Reward yourself when you find these ways are saving you rainy-day dollars.

In short, be proactive to rainy-day planning, not

reactive when it's too late. But don't let the "save for a rainy-day" theorists make your life miserable and meaningless.

FLAXSEED FACTORS TO REMEMBER

1. Decide to have a balanced approach to saving money, so you can live your life to the fullest . . . and not look back someday, depressed about how you missed out on so many fun things.

2. Don't be obsessed with the edict "save, save, save." Don't be obsessively frugal. Yes, save a good deal of money, but don't save it all. Go out and enjoy it.

3. Dismiss the feeling of guilt the moment it sets in. Push back and get it out of your head. We all feel a little guilty spending big bucks on a fabulous vacation. Or on an overpriced vehicle. But it's worth it, and the memories usually outweigh the cost.

4. So, when you're about to spend money, but suddenly feel guilty about it, tell yourself to end the thought at this very moment, and go spend it. It can bring joy and very pleasant memories to you and your family . . . and you can't put a price tag on those memories.

5. Consider the many ways you can save money without being too frugal or cheap. Use a financial planning expert to help guide you on how to be ready for retirement. It's worth what it costs if you find an effective, savvy, experienced planner.

6. Just take a deep breath, let go, spend and enjoy. That's what the money is there for.

Part Three
Communication

Communication is fundamental. As *Merriam-Webster's Collegiate Dictionary* describes it, communication is "a process by which information is exchanged between individuals through a common system of symbols, signs, or behaviors."[12] It's the foundation of people surviving in this continuously challenging world.

How we communicate and how effective we are in doing it can make or break who we are as successful, confident individuals. Shockingly, as important as communication is, it's not a required course in education and, therefore, only a small percentage of people learn how to apply and master it effectively.

One thing is for sure: An effective communicator can deal with and relate to different kinds of people in a positive, tactful, productive way. Empathy, energy, clarity, and credibility are some of the key components that make that happen. And listening is so relevant to good, effective communication. How many people have been trained in listening? The number is tiny.

This section of *Forget That!* tackles several aspects of communication that we deal with frequently but might have been misadvised about. We were taught or acquired incorrect lessons and are about to unlearn them.

Serious stuff, but not rocket science. The key thing is to try relating to each one of these mistruths, think about them in terms of your particular life and experiences, and, going forward, incorporate the things that work for you.

Eleven
Lesson to Unlearn #11
The More, the Better

More isn't better in many cases. Forget that!

"Less is more" often makes much better sense than "more is better."

"The more you say, the more you know" is a mistruth. The truth is . . . the more people hear you ramble, the less they want to be around you. It's so much easier to like people rather than dislike them. So much more fun to enjoy others, versus being turned off by them. And much more positive to be engaged with others versus removed and detached.

All of this begins and ends with communication. Every communication usually consists of at least one sender and one or more receivers.

Regarding written communications, it is a delusion that writing more suggests you know more about a topic.

The idea that the wordier you are, the smarter you come across, is nonsense. It's usually just the opposite! Kids still try fooling the teacher by writing more than they need to write, but that doesn't work. Good, concise, clear written communication filled with facts is the way to go.

Nevertheless, people ramble on and on and take forever to make their point, making us want to push a button and disappear.

I remember in high school and college, before the world became digitized, students got blue books for exams. You had to write your answers in a sixteen-page blue book, and the perception was, the more you wrote, the higher the grade you would receive. So, we'd all try filling up the blue book with verbiage just because more seemed better. On some occasions, we'd hear a classmate ask the teacher, "Can I have another blue book?" and the kids would shudder. "Holy cow! She's on her second blue book, and she obviously knows much more than I know."

I vividly remember one day taking a major exam. One girl asked for another blue book because she had filled up all sixteen pages of the first blue book. You could hear the moans in the room. We were stunned. "Give me a break—she's on her second blue book, and I'm only on page nine of my first. I'm screwed and going to fail this test!"

I call this verbosity "Blue Book Disease." That is . . . the longer the written communication, the more people think you know what you are talking about. But do they really? It can be just the opposite—the more succinct you are, the more thought they give to your message. Plus, remember that people have plenty of other reading to do, and your written communication might not be a priority.

Many people are long-winded and verbose when they speak and write. And the listeners or readers get so turned off they skim the written document or fake attention with the verbal message.

This "blue book" habit rubbed off on some people when they became adults and went to work. We see this every day with the countless emails and texts we receive. Most of them must be skimmed because they're too long and there's not enough time to read them all. More is not better. Less is more!

And listeners, who are faking attention in many cases because the speaker is verbose and disconnected, just roll their eyes and pretend they're listening. They stop listening and think about what they want to say or ascribe their own opinions on what's being said. Or they mentally disappear.

They've heard enough.

Leslie Moore doesn't know when to stop. He thinks that his oral presentations have to contain countless pieces of supportive data, example after example after example. More than a slide a minute—it's torture to be in Les Moore's audience.

People get the message early on. But he's still up there preaching everything he knows about the subject, and using painfully busy slides, often in tiny, illegible print, to drive home a point that has already been made.

And the group he had won over from the start is now turned off, bored, dozing off, or sending texts.

Leslie Moore took a positive skill he possessed and turned it into a negative, because he thought that more was better. He had learned that myth from the first boss in his early twenties, who reamed him out for not being thorough enough. His boss reprimanded him because he didn't have enough slides, and the slides he did use were too short and not detailed enough.

People dreaded going to Les Moore's presentations. When they saw him in the hallway, they walked the other way, especially if they had a meeting to attend. They feared that he could take a fifteen-second communication and turn it into fifteen painful, rambling minutes.

One day, a senior leader read him the riot act in a half serious, half kidding way. He told Leslie he might be the smartest guy in the room, but people want to leave the room in fear he'll ramble on. A reputation like that wasn't helping his career at all. Leslie got the message loud and clear, and finally became self-aware.

On the contrary, Art Tikulitt is the most concise,

crisp, no-nonsense speaker in the world. He makes his point quickly and decisively, then stops. He allows the other person to speak, even more than he speaks. People love being with him, and always get it. And they end up doing most of the speaking.

No shock that Art became the CEO of one of the world's leading companies. "Less is more" continues to be his verbal and written communication style.

APPLYING THIS TO REAL LIFE

If you can say something in fewer words, do so. If you can write it in fewer words, go for it. Leslie Moore types of communication get you nowhere.

If you've made your point and accomplished your objective in communicating, stop there. Let it sink into the other person's head. Don't overtalk, overstate, or overkill.

People get it, usually. And if they don't, then perhaps repeat your main idea, or ask them if they have any questions about what you said or wrote. Or pause. If they have questions, the power of the pause usually gets them to speak, or at least digest what you have just said.

The "less is more" theory applies to many other things. Less stuff in your home means more space to live in. Less social media means more time to do productive things. Less booze means more sleep (usually). Fewer words mean more.

FLAXSEED FACTORS TO REMEMBER

1. Conciseness always rules!

2. Eliminate unnecessary words. People don't think you're smarter just because you say a lot.

3. In many cases, people are even more impressed if you gather your thoughts and express them as concisely and decisively as possible.

4. One game I play with my clients is the "wasted words" game. When they send me a sample of an important proposal or general written communication and want feedback, I count the unnecessary words and charge them fifty cents for every gratuitous, dispensable word or phrase. They then must donate that money to a charity.

Twelve

Lesson to Unlearn #12

Use Formal Language in Business Communication

If I looked you in the eye and said, "Please be advised that I will not be in the office tomorrow," would you wonder if I was weird, using the words "Please be advised that?"

Of course you would!

Would you, yourself, ever tell a person, "Please be advised that I am purchasing a new laptop in the not-too-distant future."

Of course you wouldn't.

The person would look you in the eyes and think you were peculiar, bizarre, or from another planet.

And if you heard yourself recorded using that inane language, you'd be shocked to hear yourself talk that way. Even worse, you'd be humiliated.

Instead, you might simply say, "I am purchasing a new laptop this year."

As simple as that.

Or another hackneyed example. Would you ever say to a person, "It has recently come to my attention that we have a serious financial problem regarding . . ."?

I doubt it. You'd probably say, "We have a serious financial problem regarding . . ." You said it in seven words, not fifteen. You omitted the words, "It has recently come to my attention that . . ."

And finally, would you begin an email or formal letter with the words, "I am writing this email to inform you that . . ."?

Must you tell the reader that you "are writing an email to inform them"? Don't they realize that you are, in fact, writing to them? Don't you think they can surmise that you are informing them? Why else would you be writing?

Why do some people say "that said" or "having said that" when you are about to say something and remind a person that you had just said something? Sounds redundant, gratuitous, and even silly to me.

As are the words "at this point in time" when you could use one word: "Now."

What's my point?

Once upon a time, when we were beginning to work or even before that, we heard some people use language we had never heard before or used ourselves.

It was as if it had come from another world. It seemed

like an odd, eccentric way to communicate. Even bizarre, because who would ever speak that way in person?

So, what did we do? We adopted that same absurd, unclear, bizarre language into our business vocabulary.

And when we wrote emails or other communications, we wrote differently than we spoke.

We adopted that silly language, as weak, peculiar, and unclear as it was, because that's the way the older, more experienced people wrote.

Hackneyed, overused, and trite expressions and phrases entered our lives without us really being aware of how senseless and insipid they were. They just snuck into our business vocabulary.

Well, the lesson here is simple.

Don't impress! Express!

Don't use written communication to show how smart or articulate you are. Use it to express your message as clearly and concisely as possible. If you'd be embarrassed to say it, don't write it.

Remove hackneyed, overused, banal, weak expressions, phrases, and words when you write and speak. They do nothing for you and your communication!

What's a hackneyed, banal expression?

It's an overused, commonplace, usually wordy and indecisive phrase that is worn-out. People use the expression repeatedly, and it's lost its meaning and impact.

Or as I call it, it's "Trite Talk."

It's lost all meaning because it's been used so much. It's cliché!

Ban Trite Talk from your communicating. Simple as that.

Here are common examples of Trite Talk. Which of these do you find yourself speaking or writing?

As soon as possible: What does that really mean? It means nothing. What might be "as soon as possible" for you might be later, not sooner, for them. It's implicit, not explicit, and confuses recipients. Instead, be specific with dates and exact action steps. Only say "as soon as possible" when that's what you mean and have no deadline or timeframe for action.

At your earliest convenience: What might be convenient for you might not be convenient for them, or vice versa. It's a lazy, indecisive way of requesting something without being explicit and exact. Prohibit it from your everyday language. It's vague and creates confusion.

At this point in time: That Trite Talk phrase tops the charts. It's said millions of times a day. Why not just say "now" or "presently"?

We're on the same page: What are we . . . books or sheets of paper? Yes, I know it's handy to use that expression, but it's become banal, cliché, even platitudinous. Don't you mean "we agree" or something more specific?

That being said: Don't you love it when somebody tells you something, and right after they tell you it, they subsequently say "that being said" or "that said" or "having said that."

As you know, or, **as you are well aware**: Well, if I know, or am well aware, then why are you telling me? They're both hackneyed expressions that can be annoying and offensive. When you tell a person, "As you are aware," they wonder what your real intention or hidden agenda is. Are you covering your rear end just in case a problem surfaces in the future and you want people to know that you told them so?

Thanking you in advance, or **thanks in advance**: You would never speak that sentence face-to-face to a person, so why write it? If you used that language in person, people would think you're peculiar, or even passive-aggressive. And how do you thank a person in advance anyway? "Beau, thanking you in advance for sending me the analytics report." Beau would look at you like you were from the moon. Or worse, "Thanking you in advance for sending me the analytics reports, I remain sincerely yours." Hard to believe that some people still say, "Sincerely yours." Are you theirs?

If you should have any further questions, please don't hesitate to contact me: That's one of the most common, trite sentences to end a communication, and it's also wordy and sounds like a form letter. Just say, "If you have questions, please contact me." Or "Please contact me if you have questions." Believe me, they'll contact you if they have questions, or don't like what they've read. They don't need to read that trite closing.

I am writing this email to inform you that: Do you have to tell them that you're writing an email? Can't they see that for themselves?

To make a long story short: Oh! If you must tell them that, your story is probably too long to start with. Just say it concisely and don't tell them you're making it short.

To be perfectly honest with you: Does that mean that up to now, you haven't been honest with them? You've lied to them?

For your information: Isn't it obvious that what you're writing or saying is for their information? If it's not for their information, then what's it intended for, or who's it for?

Immediately: You might think that this word is fine, but it really isn't. "Immediately" to you might mean today, or right now. "Immediately" to them might be this week, this month, or this year . . . or worse, when I have the time to get to it. It's vague and weak. Say exactly what you mean, don't imply it. Use a date to be explicit. But be polite and not abruptly demanding.

Think outside the box: Twenty-five years ago, it was cool, original . . . but now it's exhausted. Ditto "out of the box."

Strictly between you and me: Yeah, right! Most

of the time, it's "between you and me, and the other people I tell."

To be frank with you: Versus "To be vague, deceitful, or full of it"? Just be frank and forthright—no need to tell them that you're being frank.

Low-hanging fruit: Another exhausting phrase. The low-hanging fruit may be tempting, but climbing higher and stretching for higher branches might be more rewarding.

Don't have the bandwidth: What a cliché that is! Bandwidth is "the transmissions capacity of an electronic device." Is that what you mean?

Bottom line impact: The bottom line is . . . so overused and trite that rarely do people take those words seriously. Around forty years ago, it had meaning.

Win-win scenario: Is it really mutually beneficial and satisfying to all?

For your perusal, attention, or action: Perusal? Must they be told that?

Value added: Aha! So, will they receive something for little or no incremental cost?

Unique: Who says so? Is there research that supports that?

Totally unique: What's the difference between unique and totally unique?

Best in class: Who determined and decided that? Potential school valedictorian?

Let's take this offline: What? The conversation, the meeting—are we online?

Cutting edge: Of what? Truly a fact, or hype? And where's the documentation that supports that it's cutting edge?

Exceed expectations: Often it is hype; set objectives and clearly meet them. Be specific.

Consensus of opinion: Redundant. A consensus is defined as "a collective opinion." A consensus of opinion and a collective opinion? All in one sentence?

Let's cut to the chase: Oh! Have we been rambling or evasive up to now?

And finally, the worst and most trite one of all . . . the one that we globally hear 800,000 times an hour . . .

It is what it is! How many times have you heard that expression?

. . . and the list goes on and on.

So, the next time you're about to use overused, worn-out language, give some thought to saying it more originally, more explicitly . . . or not at all. Or read this chapter again.

"That being said" . . . get rid of all that Trite Talk.

APPLYING THIS TO REAL LIFE

When you have a few minutes, look at the last fifty to one hundred written communications you've sent out.

Emails, letters, reports, proposals . . . anything where you had to give information, express yourself, or persuade or influence the other person to accept your idea, service, or product.

Review each communication like your staunch English teacher would have done when you were completing an essay or report.

Put a red line through every word that isn't necessary. Delete words that have little or no impact or provide no additional clarity.

Delete anything that is so pompous, trite, or hackneyed that the reader could be potentially turned off, or think you were bizarre for writing it.

Now take a look at what the written communication looks like. Look at all the red lines that go through the words and phrases/sentences.

And the next time you're composing something, keep asking yourself . . . would I speak that way if the person was with me face-to-face? Would they look at me like I was peculiar or insane? Or just boring?

Write the same way you speak.

FLAXSEED FACTORS TO REMEMBER

1. We tend to speak with worn-out expressions and clichés that have lost impact and originality over the years. Most of the time, we're even unaware that we're using that language.

2. Avoid overused, hackneyed Trite Talk. It does nothing for you and can be annoying or confusing to the other person.

3. If you're not sure whether something sounds hackneyed or trite, try speaking it to yourself. Would you say that aloud to another human if you spoke with them in person or over the phone? That's the litmus test. You'll quickly break that bad habit.

4. Realize the other person might not react to or give you feedback about your overuse of clichés and Trite Talk. But they are hearing it and formulating an impression of you. And it's not a very good one.

5. Buzz phrases like "It is what it is" or "At the end of the day," as a rule, say nothing. They subliminally tell the recipient that you are trite and lack originality. Who needs that reputation! Be mindful that we are always being judged by other people, and the words we communicate with are a major part of that judgment.

Thirteen

Lesson to Unlearn #13

Listen as Much as You Speak

Forget that! You should listen **four times** more than you speak, not just "as much as you speak."

In my seminars and coaching engagements, one of the first things I teach my clients is the 80-20 Rule of Life.

You should listen 80 percent of the time, and speak 20 percent, maximum. You don't need to speak any more than that, although most people do.

And not just at work or home, but in life. Not just from nine to five, but from five to nine. With friends, family, colleagues . . . and most importantly, with your spouse and in parenting.

Even when you're giving an oral presentation, you shouldn't do all the speaking. Involve the audience in the talk, ask hypothetical or rhetorical questions. Even if they don't get involved verbally, they get involved mentally. Get the wheels turning in their heads.

I was the keynote speaker at Burger King's franchise conference years back, and although there were around three thousand people in the audience, I geared my presentation around their total involvement and their mental WIIFM (what's in it for me). And for half the presentation, I strolled around the audience getting them involved.

That's why I call it the "80-20 Rule of Life." **Listen four times more than you speak**. Be a truly active listener 365 days a year. Not only at work, but everywhere you go. Even the dentist's office.

During that 20 percent of your speaking, you'll have more than enough time to get your point across, and people will respect and appreciate you for it. That's a key point. You're giving them a chance to do most of the speaking, and that goes a long way in relationship building.

Most people love to talk. Not just extroverts, but quiet, introverted people also. Get them started and watch what happens!

And quiet, shy kids often want to talk more than you realize. It just doesn't come naturally. Give them something that has WIIFM (what's in it for me) in it, and that often opens them up to speak about WIIFM.

Frank De Yentah was a genius. He had several advanced degrees, was Phi Beta Kappa, top of his class, had post-docs and fellowships, the list goes on and on. And De Yentah spoke beautifully. He was articulate, fluid, dynamic. A real fireball. That was the good news!

The bad news was that he never shut up. Never stopped talking.

He broke all the listening rules. Dominated all conversations. Never missed an interruption when he sensed he could dive in and take over. He was the consummate "authority" on everything, even on things he didn't know.

Frank barely listened, and when he did, you could tell he couldn't wait until you were done. He faked attention and daydreamed. His reactions when people spoke were really aimed at just trying to get them to hurry up and finish what they had to say. He wanted to get back on center stage and do the speaking, not the listening, which he had no time or patience for.

Everybody sensed that. They liked him superficially, respected his great knowledge and background, but deep down, they detested him. Respected his work but nothing else.

His supervisor begged him to listen more and speak less, but he just couldn't. He always had to let you know how intelligent he was and prove he was the smartest guy in the room.

One day, out of nowhere, he was demoted and was

never told why. Some contrived excuses were given.

He never recovered from that traumatic blow. Down went his confidence. Down went his following—they couldn't take him anymore. Down went his career. And he claimed he was oblivious to this negative trait.

Very sad story . . . because all his followers left Frank, and so did his wife. There are millions of people in the world that are like Mr. De Yentah. They ramble on and on with no desire to stop, and when they do and the other person says something, they interrupt them in the first or second sentence.

Harry Curleytoe was just the opposite. He listened until you couldn't speak anymore. He asked questions about what you were saying. He commented on what you were describing and then asked more questions that got you to continue. He was genuinely interested in the other person and what they had to say, not what he had to say.

And everybody adored Harry, including his boss, who got him promoted to vice president before he turned thirty. He wasn't a rocket scientist, but he got an A+ in listening.

Freddy Connermann was a very interesting listener. Yes, he was an active listener, but he used listening as a persuasive tool, and blatantly attempted to use it to con people. He read a book or two about the power of exceptional listening, but used it in a manipulative, passive-aggressive way.

It didn't take people long to figure out that his listening was an act. He was conning people by letting them talk, talk, talk, and then delivering the purpose point. But that's only a bad example; please keep the positive examples in mind as you set your goal to become a much better listener.

APPLYING THIS TO REAL LIFE

It's as simple as this: The more you listen, the more people like you. They appreciate you and want to be around you. They believe in you and follow you.

And the more you listen, the more you learn.

Conversely, the more you speak, especially when you go on and on, the more they wish you'd shut up.

Listening is the silent motivator. It takes no education or training to get an A+ in listening. And it's worth more than most of the other grades you get.

Here is a list of "Bad Listening" habits that millions of people are guilty of. Rate yourself between 10 and 1 (10 being the worst score; 1 being the best score). The lower the total score, the better. The habits are not in any ranking of badness. They're all glowingly bad.

And be honest with yourself—this exercise can have a major impact on your personal and professional life, if you take it to heart. Some people tell me it's a life changer, including at home.

	BAD LISTENING HABIT	Your Self-Rating Score
1	Interrupting—Jumping in before they're done speaking 10 9 8 7 6 5 4 3 2 1	
2	Closed-mindedness—Nobody's going to change me 10 9 8 7 6 5 4 3 2 1	
3	Assuming—Assuming something with few or no facts (ASSUME—Could stand for "make an **ass** of **you** and **me**") 10 9 8 7 6 5 4 3 2 1	
4	Faking attention—Making believe you're listening 10 9 8 7 6 5 4 3 2 1	
5	Tolerating/allowing distractions 10 9 8 7 6 5 4 3 2 1	
6	Daydreaming—You're mentally somewhere else 10 9 8 7 6 5 4 3 2 1	
7	Coaxing/nudging them verbally or nonverbally to finish up 10 9 8 7 6 5 4 3 2 1	
8	Jumping to quick, unfounded conclusions 10 9 8 7 6 5 4 3 2 1	

9	Emotional listening—being triggered by an emotion-laden word or phrase **10 9 8 7 6 5 4 3 2 1**	
10	Blind listening—Ignoring their body language and tone of voice **10 9 8 7 6 5 4 3 2 1**	
11	Making false inferences—not listening between the lines correctly **10 9 8 7 6 5 4 3 2 1**	
12	Getting overstimulated, emoted by the message **10 9 8 7 6 5 4 3 2 1**	
13	Thinking only about what you want to say **10 9 8 7 6 5 4 3 2 1**	
14	Judging their delivery while speaking **10 9 8 7 6 5 4 3 2 1**	
15	Prejudging—Preserving our ways of thinking and avoiding being convinced of something different **10 9 8 7 6 5 4 3 2 1**	
16	Dismissing—concluding early on that the subject is not interesting **10 9 8 7 6 5 4 3 2 1**	

17	Writing down every word possible and missing so much by doing so **10 9 8 7 6 5 4 3 2 1**	
18	Doing something else with your mind while listening **10 9 8 7 6 5 4 3 2 1**	
19	Monopolizing the conversation **10 9 8 7 6 5 4 3 2 1**	
20	Passive listening—Hearing somebody speak, or something said, but not being 100 percent attentive **10 9 8 7 6 5 4 3 2 1**	

SCORING	
20-34	You are an awesome listener; kudos and congrats. Why not consider teaching a course in active listening?
35-49	Solid score; you're a strong listener with just a few things to focus on and fine-tune. Good job, my friend!
50-64	Much better than the average listener; revisit the higher scores, though, and work on improving these areas.
65-7	Time to take a good, solid look at how you can improve, but this score is nothing to be ashamed of.

80-94	An OK score, but if you're striving to reach the sky, listening training could certainly help you attain that goal.
95-109	Read this chapter again and establish an action plan for yourself; effective listening training and improvement is clearly a priority. Don't put it off.
110 and higher	Go online and find either a listening skills trainer or a communications coach; your listening, or lack thereof, is hurting you. Make this exercise an opportunity for growth. It will come back in spades if you allow it to happen. Good luck and get listening.

So, how'd you do?

Some of those bad listening habits probably hit home, right? Some didn't. But hopefully they all helped you think about the critical area of effective, active listening.

Don't be discouraged if your score was fairly high. Consider this an excellent opportunity to convert lemons into lemonade, weaknesses into strengths, liabilities into opportunities. Poor listening into power listening.

And remember to live by the 80-20 Rule of Life. Everybody benefits.

FLAXSEED FACTORS TO REMEMBER

1. Apply the 80-20 Rule as a guideline. At work, home, with kids, with friends, strangers you meet, everyone, everywhere . . . and watch what happens. It's magical! Speak 20 percent of the time. The rest of the time, just listen.

2. Listening can also be called "silent" selling. You are establishing trust, rapport, and credibility with others. Winning people over. Building relationships. Those are just a few of the benefits of being an effective listener.

3. When you do the listening, people want to reciprocate. It's tempting to jump into the conversation, but don't. The more you listen and truly care about what they're saying, the more they want to be around you and listen in return.

4. Listening is a powerfully effective interpersonal communication skill that should be a high priority, especially if the skill isn't quite there yet.

5. Listening as much as you speak isn't enough. Listening around four times more than you speak is the key. People will greatly appreciate you for being a good, attentive listener, and you'll learn more.

6. Take the Bad Listening test again in six months, after this self-awareness exercise or some training. See if you have improved. If you still haven't, write down the lowest scores and put it up on your wall as an everyday reminder.

7. If you're trying to sell something or persuade or influence a person, being a great listener is a sales tool. The more you're actively listening, the more you're unobtrusively selling.

Fourteen

Lesson to Unlearn #14

Don't Criticize People

Find me a person who enjoys giving criticism to others, and you've found me a sadist.

Find me a person who enjoys receiving criticism, and you've found me a chump.

Nobody likes to receive criticism. Yes, there are many thick-skinned people in this world who can handle it, but come on—who likes to hear about their weaknesses or flaws?

Receiving negative feedback is uncomfortable, to say the least, and painful, to say the most. But giving a person criticism when it is needed is essential and a fact of life at home or work, especially if you manage people.

When I was a kid, I resented being criticized. Maybe it was because I was insecure and trying to figure it all out. Or maybe it was because of the threatening, punishing tone of voice the person often had when giving the criticism. It hurt.

I remember vividly—one time, playing on a football team, I dropped a touchdown pass. It would have been a touchdown that would have put us in the lead, but I took my eye off the ball and dropped it.

My coach, Mr. Stallworth, in front of the kids, parents and everybody else, screamed so loud at me that the opposing coach almost had to quiet him down. I was beyond hurt. I was shocked and totally embarrassed by his reprimand and sulked the rest of the game. And that was the last year I played organized team football.

My dad, God bless his soul, would give me criticism even after I would win a major tennis match. He would point out all the things I could have done better, but in an angry, kind of annoyed way. I'd always feel like crap after the criticism but knew he didn't mean harm by it, even though it depressed me.

As I grew up, however, I realized that criticism, when given constructively, factually, and carefully, is actually a gift. More than a gift, a must! So, I began to welcome it, and to this day, very much still do.

And when I occasionally had to deliver criticism to another person, it was uncomfortable and tough to do. I tried hard to be careful, not to offend or upset them, but to genuinely try to help them via the feedback. But man, it was stressful.

Little did I know that someday, I would be training adults in seminars on techniques on how to constructively criticize, motivate, and coach others. Helping to develop other people in a motivational, inspiring, goal-driven way.

The fact is that very few people, if any, gain pleasure or satisfaction giving negative feedback to people. It's not easy to give negative feedback, and as you're delivering it, you often detect the uneasiness and pain of the person receiving it. Or worse, their defensiveness.

But in business and life it's very important to be able to give people critical, constructive feedback when it's needed. And for most people, it's not easy to do.

I don't like the sound and the implications of the word "criticism," so let's change the name to "motivational criticism," or even "motivational feedback."

That name has a better ring to it, and more importantly, describes in two words what you're attempting to accomplish—giving the person constructive, sometimes painful feedback, but in a motivational, positive, potentially life-changing way.

MOTIVATIONAL CRITICISM DEFINED

So, what do I mean by "motivational criticism," a term I coined when I started my consulting firm, Motivational Systems, Inc., decades ago?

It's motivational feedback where the person feels helped, not hurt. Constructive, motivational communication helps convert a person's negatives and challenges into positives, opportunities, and goals.

More than just criticism, it's information that inspires, motivates, and energizes a person to improve in a particular area. It's geared to motivate people to raise their performance and grow substantially.

It's not "reprimanding" the person, a term most people despise. *Merriam-Webster's Collegiate Dictionary* defines the verb "reprimand" as "to reprove sharply or censure formally usually from a position of authority."[13]

Just the opposite of what motivational criticism is, although some folks confuse the two terms. Eliminate the word "reprimand" from your vocabulary and leadership tool kit. Substitute it with "motivational criticism," which is needed by everybody who wants to keep growing and developing.

Few people enjoy criticizing others. But few know how to do it the right way, meaningfully. There's no satisfaction in criticizing unless you are coaching, developing, and improving that person. That's when criticism becomes wonderful, a gift, and a genuine developmental tool.

Let's adopt that philosophy and incorporate it into our everyday lives. The lesson to unlearn is to think that giving criticism is a negative. In essence, it's a real positive when done effectively.

ONE THING THAT IS COMMON FOR EVERYBODY: WE ALL NEED TO GROW

Whether they know it or not, every person in this world needs to grow and feel like they're continuing to develop.

That's part of one's self-actualization, and unless people feel like they're self-actualizing, they feel like they're stuck in a swamp or quicksand. And that could be demotivating, demoralizing, and even depressing.

That's why retirement is often tough for many people, especially those who have had a successful, rewarding, busy career. They suddenly awaken retired one morning with no goals, no objectives for that day, not much to do, and at the end of that day, they feel like they have accomplished little or nothing.

Whenever I vacation in Florida, I always meet several retired people who have moved to Florida to live their next chapter of life. Most tell me that they wish they hadn't retired that early because they feel unmotivated, unchallenged, and even brain-dead. They have few or no goals and not much to strive for, other than a sunny day.

We all need self-actualization, recognition, and the feeling of accomplishment.

Motivational criticism helps fulfill that important goal because its purpose is to enhance a person's self-actualization. It's a critical leadership skill to possess, yet some people avoid it. Or when they do it, they either fail to meet the mark or screw up tremendously. Who is the recipient of this failure? The person being criticized.

CLUELESS IN GIVING CRITICAL FEEDBACK: A VERY PAINFUL EXAMPLE

I certainly didn't have the skill of giving effective criticism when I was a young upstart launching a brand-new consulting business. And I detested doing it. I put my foot in my mouth a few times when I had to level with a person about areas I felt they weren't performing well in, and where they needed to improve.

But how quickly I learned . . . the hard way. One incident stands out vividly, and to this day, very painfully.

Miles Mathews, one of my finest employees ever and as dedicated as they came, did outstanding training and consulting work for my firm, and was recognized and rewarded nicely for it.

But one time, he totally screwed up with a major

client, inadvertently insulting the person. He asked the client a question in front of a large group, and surprisingly the client didn't know the answer. He had no clue.

Miles, instead of just acknowledging that instance and moving forward, remarked to the client that he was shocked to hear that the client had no idea what he was talking about.

"I can't believe you don't know about this new Human Resources EEO ruling. It's something that everybody in our field knows was passed by the federal government."

The client, Justin Paine, quite insecure and a bit inept, was so dismayed and embarrassed at the way Miles handled him publicly that he called me that day and complained vociferously.

Mr. Paine abruptly told me that his company no longer wanted to see Miles anymore, and for us to send another consultant to do the work. He reduced the contract we had agreed upon. And he told me to keep Miles out of his company, although Miles was a proven star and just slipped and screwed up that one time.

The client was certainly way too defensive about Miles's insensitive remark, but our firm lost both the battle and the war with him.

When I spoke with Miles to hear his side of the story, I committed every communication sin in the book. Here's how I screwed up famously . . .

1. **Did it over the telephone.** A big no-no. You should never give feedback over the phone unless it is impossible to see the person face-to-face. The reason: You can't observe the way the person is taking the feedback and respond appropriately. You can't see their nonverbal reaction, and for all you know, they could be in tears, and you'd never know it. I have a feeling that Miles was in tears on the other line.

   Miles was very hurt and never got over the way I gave him that feedback, and it showed in his future work. I felt terrible, apologized profusely, and even today, decades later, I still feel awful.

2. **Criticizing a person in a room with people nearby.** These people sense what's going on, and the person being criticized becomes embarrassed or livid and turns off their listening. If there are other people nearby, take the conversation to an empty room. If you can't find one, hold off the criticism until you do. But don't wait too long. I criticized Miles over the phone, but so many times, I've seen people being criticized with other people situated nearby.

3. **Using the word "you" repeatedly.** That too is a cardinal sin in giving constructive feedback. Never use the word "you" when criticizing a

person. Get in the habit of saying the same thing but without the word "you," which makes the criticism personal and attacking, and not constructive and motivating.

Example: "Miles, I was told by Justin Paine that he was taken aback by a comment **you** made to him. Apparently, **you** totally embarrassed Justin when **you** called his attention to his ineptness. **You** obviously weren't very tactful."

Count all of those "you" words (4) and you'll see I was relentless with my feedback. This made the feedback an emotional, traumatic moment for Miles versus a productive learning experience. Avoiding the word "you" and substituting with "I" depersonalizes the criticism as much as possible, thereby making it less painful to swallow.

4. **Criticizing the person, not the problem.** Like point number three, don't find yourself criticizing the individual; speak in terms of the problem and specific incident. Describe what happened, what the damage was, the negative effect, but don't personalize it and come down on the person. Make it issue-oriented, not person-oriented.

   If you need to vent your emotions, hold them inside during the session and then go outside and run a mile or kick your tire.

Two more examples, a faulty one and a positive one, illustrate this point.

"**You** were wordy in writing the report" versus "The report was wordy." Or "**You** are late for the meeting" versus "The meeting was scheduled to begin at 10 a.m."

In both examples, the second iteration identified the problem and avoided criticizing the person. Eliminating the word "you" in each example goes a long way. "You" can be a very emotional word. Save it for when you're praising a person, not criticizing them.

5. **Dealing with more than one criticism.** Don't pile on and bring up another negative issue during the session. That makes the session less effective. I dropped the ball once again during that session with Miles by bringing up a previous problem that had to be addressed, but was not at all related to the main issue at hand.

6. **Raising your voice.** You should keep your voice down and not project volume and energy during the session. Use a soft, low-key voice versus a loud, energetic, enthusiastic tone. Research shows that when you keep your volume down in a negative communication situation, you lessen the emotional

reaction to the information, and the conversation tends to go more smoothly and quickly.

7. **Taking too long to speak with the person.** You should discuss the issue immediately after it happens, or as soon as it's humanly possible. Criticize immediately, not several days or weeks later. If you criticize the person well after the incident occurred, you missed the boat and it's too late. Do everything possible to speak with the person right after you learn about it.

   Miles lived around forty miles from our office, and in hindsight, I should have asked him if he minded that I drive down to his local coffee shop and speak with him about something. I didn't do that, and subsequently missed a developmental opportunity by waiting too long to speak with him.

Other mistakes people make when criticizing:

1. **Being overly animated.** Pointing a finger when talking, losing control, and not observing or responding to the person's body language are all counterproductive and hurtful.

2. **Going on too long.** The meeting is painful enough without it going too long. Less is more!

3. **Not being empathetic, compassionate, supportive.** Even though the person cost you and your company huge dollars, show that you're still behind them 100 percent. I did in the Miles scenario, but the damage had already been done.

4. **Not ending the session on a positive.** Make sure the person knows they are still a key and important member of the team, and you respect and cherish them. This is hard to do over the phone because who knows how they're taking the feedback.

APPLYING THIS TO REAL LIFE

I felt terrible about the whole Miles criticism incident and thought about it for a long time. Realizing that I could never let that happen again, personally and professionally, I developed an eight-step model for giving effective motivational criticism.

I swear by these techniques and have taught them to countless people over the past several decades.

Here are the eight motivational criticism steps to apply:

1. **Begin the meeting with a positive statement.** Don't dive into the criticism the moment you begin the meeting. Break the ice and ease into it instead. Example: "Miles, you're one of the most

valuable consultants our firm has ever had, and I hear so much positive feedback about you."

2. **Avoid the words "but," "however," or "although."** Don't follow the opening positive remarks with the word "but" because it totally negates the complimentary opening thoughts you shared with the person. And don't use the words "however" or "although" after praising the person at the outset. Example: "Miles, you're one of the most valuable consultants our firm has, and I hear so much positive feedback about you. **But** there's a problem that occurred and you need to hear about it." Avoid the temptation of the "but" conjunction.

3. **Use the PEN acronym to present the specific criticism.**

   P stands for Problem. State the problem right up front. Get right to the point.

   E stands for Example(s). Now give examples that back up the problem that occurred. Support the point you're making with factual examples, not generalized, unrelatable comments or opinion-based thoughts.

   N stands for Negative Effects of the problem. State the negative ramifications that the problem created.

Again, make sure that you avoid the word YOU when giving this PEN feedback. You can say "You" before or after presenting PEN, but not during it.

It's a good idea to prepare the PEN informational points prior to the feedback session.

4. **Ask for feedback.** You've done enough talking up to now, so let the person respond to the PEN feedback. Don't interrupt at all, even if they're defensive or caustic. Example: "Miles, what are your thoughts about this matter?"

5. **Actively listen:** Show the person that you really care about what they are saying and how they're reacting. Don't glare or look stone-faced. Don't withhold verbal or nonverbal feedback. And never interrupt the person.

6. **Engage in a warm, open dialogue.** Show empathy and compassion. Don't speak rapidly, and use periodic pauses. That will also help remove the "you" words that you may use inadvertently.

7. **Come to a mutual understanding.** Discuss back and forth. And after you both reach a decision on a corrective, next-step plan of action, let the person

tell you exactly what they plan to do, and the timeframe. They, not you, should summarize the action steps and timeframes.

8. **End on a positive.** End with the same positive remark you opened the meeting with. Or give them another positive. Assure them there are no hard feelings and you totally support them. "Miles, I want to remind you that you're one of the most valuable people in our firm, and I greatly appreciate you." That's called the sandwich technique. Begin and end with a positive and sandwich in the negative feedback and PEN communication.

People tell me the hardest thing to do is give the PEN feedback without saying the word "you." Yes, it's difficult to do, but once you get it down, you'll stop yourself from saying the word "you" right before it's about to flow off your tongue.

Again, keep in mind that the "you" rule is for when you're delivering the specific PEN feedback, not for the entire conversation. There are times when saying "you" is the only way to say it, but try keeping "you" away from PEN, or when you don't need it.

Once you practice this eight-step technique, it'll come more naturally. At first, it'll be a bit awkward or uncomfortable. But your goal is to help, not hurt, the person, and this process can only help accomplish that objective.

Use this technique at home also. It never hurts to be tactful and motivational, but firm and decisive when leveling with a person. The goal is accomplished without hurting feelings or angering the recipient.

MOTIVATIONAL PRAISE DEFINED

I love this topic, motivational praise.

Yes, you can praise a person, that's easy . . . but you can also motivationally praise a person. There's a big difference between the two.

Praising someone can be one of the great highs for that person or it can be a letdown. Or something in between.

Sounds contradictory, but motivational praise is a wonderful opportunity to reward even more than just giving money and bonuses.

Whereas motivational criticism can be described as "constructive feedback in which the person feels helped, not hurt, and inspired, motivated, and energized in a particular area," motivational praise is the "stepsister." What do I mean?

It's the fuel that lights up the person's engine. When communicated sincerely and effectively, it can be a huge motivator and a productivity enhancer. Plus, it can help raise the performance bar of the person and motivate them to accomplish even more.

When praising a person at work, or even at home, adopt this four-step CEBG model in your delivery of the praise . . .

C—Compliment the person's accomplishment in general terms.

E—Example(s); give them an example or two of specifically what they did well. Be factual, not opinion-based.

B—Benefits; enthusiastically tell them the benefits of their accomplishment, regarding all involved or impacted people.

G—Goals; raise the bar higher for them. They're primed and energized to grow even further. So set another goal and inspire them to attain it.

Here are two examples—a weak, unmotivating one that totally misses a motivational opportunity . . . and a good, inspiring example applying the CEBG model of motivational praising.

"Dr. Lylechild, your monthly address to employees was excellent. They derived a lot from it. Good job."

Versus . . .

"Dr. Lylechild, your monthly address to your employees was excellent. They derived a lot from it (C).

"You were dynamic, articulate, highly enthusiastic,

and you personalized it to everybody in the audience (E). Your eye contact was exceptional, as you gave the impression that you were looking at everybody and truly cared about them (E). And your body language and nonverbal gestures told a message in themselves (E).

"This type of motivational speech inspires your people to raise the bar even higher and establish stretch goals for themselves and the company (B).

"Here's a suggestion: Why don't you take people aside in the future and teach them your techniques of high-impact, powerful oral presentations? They will grow from that coaching and the company will be the beneficiary. What do you think? (G)"

Now take a look at the first example, a two-sentence lip service praising. It did nothing for the person, whereas the second example not only praised the person but gave an inspiring message to take the praise to the next level.

In sum, remember CEBG the next time you're praising another individual. And keep these additional six points in mind when you're praising people in general.

1. **Avoid praising people in public** when others there feel that they didn't have the same opportunity. Do it privately unless the praise will set a good example for everybody and be motivating.

2. **Don't praise unnecessarily.** Too much praising defeats the recognitional and motivational purpose of praising.

3. **Don't praise the obvious.**

4. **Try praising everybody.** Not at the same time, of course, but periodically find the time to extol praise for people's achievements. This goes a long way.

5. **Motivational goals** can be personal or team-driven, project-based, educational, technical, career-oriented. It's an opportunity to build up and develop your people.

6. **Giving motivational praise to a person can raise the performance bar** of that person and elicit more professional development and growth. And people greatly appreciate it!

Now that you're a motivational whiz, go out and apply these development tools.

Yes, criticism is a challenging art to master, but sorely needed for a person's personal and professional growth.

And praising people goes a long way. Just think how you feel when being praised by a person!

FLAXSEED FACTORS TO REMEMBER

1. Giving a person negative feedback is never easy, and never fun, but there's a technique for effectively doing it, motivational criticism.

2. As a leader, it's essential to learn and apply the technique of giving motivational criticism to your colleagues.

3. Feedback isn't what makes them grow, but motivational feedback is. Feedback that teaches, motivates, inspires, and establishes goals for improvement.

4. Criticize the problem, not the person. And avoid using the word "you" when citing the problem. The word "you" can take the session from constructive, motivational feedback to a personal, potentially threatening level.

5. Always criticize in person, and never over the phone. Face-to-face is a must so you can observe their nonverbal reactions.

6. Begin and end with a positive. Make sure they know your goal was to help, not hurt, and professionally develop them. And cover only one

criticism per session. Never pile on with two or more specific criticisms.

7. Yes, criticizing people is challenging, but motivationally criticizing people is extremely beneficial for all parties involved.

8. Motivational praise is an opportunity to pat a person on the back and to initiate further personal or professional growth. Use the CEBG praise model to deliver inspiring praise that raises the bar for that person.

9. Be a walking manager, regularly supporting, coaching and advising your employees when necessary, and building your relationship with them. But master the art of giving motivational feedback to people when it's appropriate. Make it part of your everyday communication style, personally and professionally.

10. Keep a weekly notebook on how many times you give negative feedback to a person using the painful word "you." Eventually, that list should be empty—you're giving motivational feedback to people. Kudos and congrats!

Fifteen

Lesson to Unlearn #15

The Best Way to Negotiate Is to Say, "Take It or Leave It!"

It's amusing when one person gives another person the "take it or leave it" ultimatum. How many times have you heard that purported threat?

Guess what! Those words usually mean they want you more than they let on, and their quasi-bullying communication is a sign of weakness or arrogance, and often both. People usually see through that put-on drama.

I remember when growing up, those words were usually an indication the other person was showing their hand, a weak signal.

When you tell a person to take it or leave it, you're actually threatening them a bit.

"Accept it or don't, but that's where I stand, and I have no interest in discussing any alternatives."

After they tell you this, and you say, "I guess I'll

leave it," you see that their threat to move on is all smoke, as they suddenly back off and even bend a little . . . or a lot.

Ludicrous, but not as much as a parent saying, "If you don't do your homework, you're not coming with us on vacation." Sure!

The expression, according to BookBrowse, emanates from the sixteenth century, when a British livery stable owner, Thomas Hobson, told people that they could either take (buy) that horse in the stable nearest the door, or leave it.[14] But it actually goes as far back as the fourteenth century and is mentioned in William Shakespeare's plays.

This expression should be outlawed from your vocabulary. It's as weak as the expression "Your bark is louder than your bite" and other outdated verbal threats.

When you tell someone to "take it or leave it," you are, in essence, saying they can accept it or not but there are no other alternatives. That's usually hogwash because you don't really mean that, and you've probably lessened your credibility with the person. There are other alternatives.

Other threatening phrases you should delete from your vocabulary are "accept it or not," "deal or no deal," "use it or lose it," and "fish or cut bait." All are win-lose expressions that could be said in better, more constructive ways.

Dee Barker was a shrewd real estate sales professional

who had a solid track record of success. But often, Dee would negotiate too hard with people and then tell them, "This is my final offer; take it or leave it."

One day, Dee was trying to buy an office building but became frustrated because the other party wouldn't budge on the final offer.

Deep down in Dee's heart, she desperately wanted to make this deal happen and would give in a bit more, if necessary. But in frustration, she told the other party to "take it or leave it; this is my final offer." The other person heard that thoughtless threat and said, "I'll leave it, thank you. Nothing more to say."

Dee realized that the deal was floating away or even gone. She regretted saying those threatening words. So, she backed off and started to give in more.

But the other person was so taken aback by her quick temper and verbal threat, she said her interest in dealing with Dee was gone. There was another prospect she was interested in doing the deal with and there was nothing else to discuss. Ouch!

Dee panicked at the response and not only backed off but offered more than she had originally planned. Still, the other person said, "I really have nothing to say because you have turned me off with your threat, let's not talk anymore."

Ballgame over—the deal fell apart and Dee was left with nothing. She was devastated.

I was seriously considering buying an office building which I thought was a bit overpriced, but something I really wanted.

The seller and I met and negotiated a price that I felt was around 10–15 percent higher than the building's worth. He told me to either "take it or leave it," and did it in such an arrogant way that I said, "Thanks, but I'm out of here."

The deal was off, the negotiations were stopped . . . and the building never sold. Incidentally, it's still for sale, many years later!

A NICER WAY TO SAY IT

As a starter, the simple, direct phrase "That's all I can do" expresses exactly what you mean, but in a nicer, more professional, less abrasive way. It's certainly less harsh than "take it or leave it," and it doesn't imply that you are through negotiating and taking things off the table.

You don't want to create lose-lose animosity with the other person, which you might regret later. Instead, you are letting them know that you've simply drawn your line and that's as far as you can go. Followed by a power pause, this is a good ploy to use.

Who knows! The other person might respect you even more and feel a bit guilty because you're such a good person about this. And they might counter with a great offer that's hard to turn down.

All much better than being contentious or nasty.

Turning the tables around, what if the other person tells you, "That's all I can do" or "take it or leave it"?

Don't take that as anything more than talk. Have them tell you what specifically that means, and why. Ask targeted questions based on their response, and if they are reluctant to respond, then it's time to ask them if this has been a waste of time. You have been direct with them but still not insulting or argumentative.

At that point, they will either step up the negotiation or leave it. But at least you're getting closure.

APPLYING THIS TO REAL LIFE

There are certain verbal habits we have that we simply must break. And one is to make rash threats that you really don't mean to people. You really can't support those inane threats, but you're trying to use them as ammunition and leverage.

Many of us did this as a kid—we'd want something from another kid who would resist it, and then we'd say, "Take it or leave it" or "S**t or get off the pot."

I remember so many times hearing the other person trying to get their way and lashing out with the passive-aggressive "take it or leave it" threat. I even remember my parents using those words to try to get me to do something.

Make up your mind that instead of using that

language, you'll try asking the other person questions about things relevant to the issue at hand.

Words like, "I'm sorry, I just can't do any better," or "That's the absolute best I can do" are much more tactful than blatant "take it or leave it" threats.

People tend to ignore ultimatums, thinking through other alternatives and even discounting your credibility. There's always the chance to continue negotiating, rather than a now-or-never mentality.

In other words, don't threaten others with win-lose language, but instead try figuring out what the problem or resistance is all about, and focus on that, not a frustrating remark that you can't back up. People see through that tactic, and it will probably come back to haunt you.

So, remove it from your thought process and catch yourself if you're about to say it. You won't regret this, especially if you want something very badly.

FLAXSEED FACTORS TO REMEMBER

1. The statement "Take it or leave it" must go. There are better, more effective things to say rather than subliminally threatening the person. It's a bad strategy and bad psychology.

2. Be specific with the language you use when at a stalemate. Words like "We seem to be at a dead

end; let's try to figure out what we must do to go forward" are much more effective than jumping to a threatening conclusion and creating a dead end.

3. The only time these words should be spoken is when you really don't want what is being discussed or offered and it truly doesn't matter to you. But then you should ask yourself why you were involved in that discussion in the first place, and perhaps move on.

4. Saying "Take it or leave it" can have repercussions in a relationship that could come back to bite you later. "What are the issues at hand?" is potentially more productive and results-driven than anything that gives off pressure, threats, and win-lose feelings to the other party.

Sixteen

Lesson to Unlearn #16

Begin a Speech with a Joke, Funny Story, Humorous Anecdote, or Witticism

That could be very dangerous. Forget that!

You might be the only person in the room who thinks that your humorous opening is entertaining. You might think the story you tell is funny and humorous, but nobody else does.

Or when you say, "Thank you for having me today," just realize that people in the audience have heard that trite, boring opening a thousand times.

I remember one time a person in the audience of a seminar I was conducting replied loud enough to be heard: "It's nice to be had." I smiled and made believe it didn't affect me. Meanwhile, as you can see, it's still in my head, decades later.

What an outdated myth this advice is. That is, to loosen up the audience with a humorous story, joke, some inane opening, or "I want to thank you!" Using icebreakers like that to open a speech is a dangerous, risky fallacy.

Whoever said we were a Larry David, Hannah Gadsby, Dave Chappelle, Hasan Minhaj, or Jim Jefferies?

Or from yesteryear, famous comics like Bob Hope, George Carlin, Richard Pryor, Jay Leno, or Eddie Murphy?

That joke or "funny" story you're planning to tell might not be that entertaining. It even might be pathetic. And you might lose the audience from the get-go and never get them back. Perhaps they've heard the joke before or are offended by it. Opening with a joke or funny story is high risk! It can damage your reputation and personal brand. At the least, it can taint your speech.

If you botch the joke, or tell the "funny" story poorly, or the humor is not so amusing, you're in serious credibility trouble with the audience, and will have a difficult time recovering from it. Or worse, you are done. And you'll subconsciously be thinking about that faux pas throughout the entire speech.

Thanking them at the speech's outset, or even worse, telling them, "What a pleasure it is to be here," is as weak and trite a beginning as you could ever come up with, except for opening with the unmotivating words "The purpose of my speech today is to . . ." That could come across as boring, insincere, and bland.

Public speaking is nerve-racking enough. Bombing

out with canned humor at the beginning of a speech amplifies that tension. And starting off by telling them, "It's a pleasure to be here today" is a yawner. Some folks moan to themselves, "Here we go again!"

I've been hearing the "begin with a joke" concept since I was a kid in school. Probably you have too. Some speech teachers and coaches are still preaching that mistruth. It's outdated public speaking theory.

I remember my speech teacher in high school telling me to open up my speech to the school with something that would relax and lighten up the audience. So, I opened it with a funny story about our tennis team sneaking into a local club pool, naked, late at night after the state tennis championships.

But the audience didn't think it was very funny. They looked at me, stone-faced, like I was from outer space. They seemed to all know it was a gimmick to open the speech. And I became nervous as hell.

Public speaking is America's #1 phobia, ahead of the fear of dying, fear of flying, and insects. It's extremely stressful and nerve-racking for most people, especially when you're opening your speech. Knees can be wobbling, hands are shaking, your heart is palpitating. Sweat is all over your body.

Many experts say that opening with a joke or funny story will lessen the tension and get you off to a good start. From their mouth to God's ears!

The dilemma is: What do you do when the joke or funny story bombs out or falls flat?

When the audience just glares at you like you're an absolute fool, as the annoying bead of sweat rolls down the side of your mortified face.

You wipe that embarrassing bead of sweat off, only to have it roll down your face once again.

Now your armpits feel like you're in a sauna bath, and your heart starts palpitating at around 133 miles an hour.

Oy! Not fun at all. You want to push a button and disappear.

You don't need hyperhidrosis (abnormally excessive sweating not related to heat or exercise) to have your nerves trigger your sweat glands to be overactive.

You just need a traumatic, joke-telling disaster.

FACT: The textbooks that profess or suggest this dated technique are wrong. Anybody who teaches you this is giving you bad advice or setting you up for potential failure. Your friends who advise you to open with a joke aren't really your friends.

Yes, professional comics, performers, and some motivational speakers are gifted joke tellers. That's how they make their livings.

They get up there, take complete control, and try to crack you up when they begin the speech. They feel like they own the audience . . . and quickly establish rapport and chemistry.

But you and I aren't professional comics. Most everyday people aren't.

We weren't born as natural comedians, and if we tell a joke and it explodes, we're dead on our feet. We've lost the audience. And we've lost initial credibility, which is so difficult to regain.

In my previous book, *No Stopping You! How to Win the Game of Life*, I had a chapter entitled "Credibility is Golden: Once You Earn it, Never Burn it." Guard credibility with your life. You could spend years building your credibility with a person or organization and then say or do one dumb thing, and boom, there goes your credibility! Guard against that. Aside from good health, family and friends, and a purpose and passion, credibility is your life!

A joke or funny story that explodes does nothing but decrease your credibility. The speech becomes a catch-up challenge. And it's traumatizing.

Bea Zarr was a phenomenal public speaker, and a pretty good joke teller. Well, at times.

At a national leadership team meeting, in front of around 1,100 upbeat, pumped-up executives and directors, she opened her motivational talk with what she thought was a hilariously funny story. It described a finance executive who rambled on and on during a presentation and had dozens of endlessly boring slides. And during her presentation, many people quietly got up and left.

Bea chuckled as she told this story, but nobody else thought it was funny. Within ten minutes of her speech, over fifty people had snuck out of the room.

FACT: First impressions are powerful, especially when presenting in front of a group of strangers. You never get a second chance to make a great first impression.

Bea's "humorous" story wasn't entertaining and motivating. It was a turnoff, and in bad taste. The expressionless faces in the room haunted her, and the stone-faced company CEO, shocked by the inappropriateness of her story, glared at her throughout the meeting.

She never recovered from that disastrous opening and never got the audience back. It was a career disaster.

Bea, of course, was never invited back. And probably never again opened a speech with a humorous story or joke. A lesson learned the traumatic way.

That experience could happen to anybody. Even to a polished presenter who mesmerizes groups all the time.

During my first year in the consulting business, I really messed up. Screwed up big time.

I opened a three-hour training session for thirty high-powered marketing people with a joke about scientists. Nobody thought it was funny. If looks could kill, I would have been dead.

There was dead silence after I told it, and after the coffee break, one-third of the attendees didn't return to the room. They were completely turned off by me and my stupid, inappropriate half-minute story, and I couldn't get them back, regardless of how hard I tried. My credibility was shot. And so was my confidence and ego that day.

That happened four decades ago, but it still hurts when I think of it. How stupid of me! But what did I know—that's what the books said to do. Complete mistruths.

A world-renowned professional athlete once opened a speech at a company's international sales meeting by telling the audience about the incredible sex he had the night before.

The speaker that day was one of baseball's all-time great sluggers. And he thought he was just being funny. His agent had advised him to warm up the audience with a humorous story at the beginning.

Dead silence ensued the next forty-five minutes after that "humorous" story. The group was shocked, repulsed. Some thought he was a derelict. Some just walked out. Hard to believe he did that.

That's an extreme example . . . but another reason why trying to be funny at the outset usually doesn't cut it.

And finally . . . a local cardiologist, Dr. Justin Hart, with one of the best reputations in the area, was running for a township office. He invited 150 people to his home to voice where he stood on local political issues.

He opened the speech with a "funny" political joke. It wasn't funny at all. It was corny. He might have been a top doc, but his joke-telling skills were a D minus! People got an immediate bad taste in their mouths and the whole evening went south for the doc after that. Many decided not to vote for him.

In sum, we're not comedians, and it's not worth the risk of beginning a speech with humor, unless you're 100 percent sure it'll work.

And who really is!

Even proven comedians tell jokes that fall flat, and they're startled. Larry David (cocreator of *Seinfeld* and creator of *Curb Your Enthusiasm*) tells this story: At a comedy club in NYC, he opened his gig with a joke, and nobody laughed. They glared. Larry got up and walked out of the building. Just like that.

The thing that most comedians do, after telling a joke or funny story that bombs out, is simply pause. They stop for seven seconds and just stare at the audience, with a doleful, meek, harmless expression on their face. And what does the audience usually do? They begin to crack up laughing because of the sudden power pause and pathetic look the comedian displays.

Unfortunately, that ploy won't work in the business world.

Don't get me wrong. Humor can be a powerful extra in a presentation. Spontaneous humor, where the funny story suddenly comes to you, usually goes over better than planned, canned humorous anecdotes or jokes.

FACT: Timing is so important with humor. When you feel the humor the very moment you're about to say it, it comes across more naturally and often works. But opening with humor is a potential red flag. A nightmare. Don't do it.

APPLYING THIS TO REAL LIFE

So how should you open a speech or presentation and avoid the humor risk?

Five different tools will help you win over the audience quickly . . .

1. **A credible shocker:** Something that might shock them but is 100 percent true.

2. **A statistic** that has a major impact. After you show the statistic, you build on it.

3. **Audience participation:** Asking a question or

questions that get people participating immediately. However, I wouldn't use this tactic with senior executives.

4. **A scenario or short story** that leads you to your presentation's purpose.

5. **A rhetorical question:** "Are you aware that . . ." Gets them thinking, engaged.

All five are much more potentially effective than a silly, irrelevant, risky joke that could turn people off and bore them.

FLAXSEED FACTORS TO REMEMBER

1. Don't open with a joke or funny story unless you are sure it'll work and is relevant to your presentation's purpose. Very risky!

2. Rarely is anyone other than a professional joke teller sure that the joke or humorous story will work as an icebreaker. Even comedians bomb out with not-so-funny jokes, but they know how to bounce right back.

3. You have little to gain with a joke or humorous story, and so much to lose if it fails. Mainly

credibility, trust, and rapport with your audience. And the joke might offend or anger some, so why take the risk?

4. Instead, open your speeches with a credible, powerful, memorable hook that . . .
    a. Stimulates the group's immediate interest
    b. Gets their attention and makes them want to listen and hear more
    c. Establishes initial rapport and chemistry with them
    d. Gives them a taste of WIIFM—"what's in it for me."

5. Giving an audience WIIFM will help accomplish your goal—to break the ice and reduce your own nervous tension, which is normal to experience. Most speakers admit to being a bit anxious at the outset of a speech.

    I've taught this WIIFM concept, "What's in it for me" globally for many decades, and it works well with people.

    They tell me that the WIIFM hook is the most important part of their speech and can make or break the rest of the presentation.

    Tune people into WIIFM and they'll tune into you.

Seventeen

Lesson to Unlearn #17

Rehearse the Speech Until You Know It Cold

I remember it like it was yesterday. I was completely traumatized.

My teacher had us all take a poem or famous speech, memorize it, and recite it for the entire class and her. We'd get graded for this memorized speech based on how effectively we gave it, how well we memorized it, and how strong our speech recital and confidence came across.

I was assigned the Gettysburg Address, Abraham Lincoln's three-minute, 272-word speech given in 1863 defining the meaning of the Civil War. I spent several weeks learning, memorizing, rehearsing, and owning the entire speech, all three long and difficult paragraphs.

The whole assignment was stressful and nerve-racking, and on my mind constantly. What if I forgot a line or two or froze up and my mind went blank?

I nailed the first two paragraphs and sailed right through. But paragraph three, in the first sentence, I lost it. Completely froze and forgot where it went. The words were . . .

"But, in a larger sense, we cannot dedicate—we cannot consecrate—we cannot hallow—this ground."[15]

From that point on, I mentally collapsed. I totally froze and forgot everything. Couldn't finish the speech because nothing came to me and was abruptly told to sit down. My knees were wobbling so much I could hardly walk back to my seat. I was sweating like it was a dog day of summer, one hundred degrees.

"You didn't study enough, Mr. Flax. You didn't take this assignment seriously, and you got a D minus grade. You better try harder next time, or I'll fail you for the marking period."

I was devastated. So were my parents, who rehearsed me repeatedly for weeks. I had given the speech to them perfectly.

I officially joined the millions of people who fear and detest public speaking and are traumatized at the thought of speech-making.

I prayed this type of assignment would never surface, although she admonished us that we'd be giving another speech in the very near future. Something that would keep me up at night.

The principle of rehearsing or memorizing a speech or presentation until you have it down pat is outlandish. Absurd. Preposterous. Asinine!

And yet, it's still often done and recommended in speech books and some training and development programs.

It's horrible, outdated advice. I've had over five decades of hands-on experience training clients on how to give spontaneous, high-impact presentations without the need for crutches like excessive notes, memorizing, podium usage, over-rehearsing, and countless slides.

I've taught thousands of people over the years that canned, over-rehearsed, crutch-dependent presentations are unnatural and undynamic. They're dangerous to a person's future career and professional development. When a person bombs out on an important oral presentation, it can have damaging effects on their credibility and subsequent success at the organization that employs them.

In my High-Impact Presentations seminars, people come to the program thinking that they must rehearse a speech like crazy, get it totally down pat in the rehearsal, even memorize it (the stupidest thing of all), and use lots of notes to guide them. They want to use a podium to hide behind and have excessive notes to guide them. All crutches.

These crutches only inhibit or remove all naturalness and spontaneity in your presentation. They make it sound contrived and not totally believable.

When you rehearse the same thing over and over, you subconsciously start to memorize the speech, which can create a new set of problems. Why? The speech, with all those rehearsals, begins to sound memorized and canned and there's a good chance that you could easily forget things you intended to say. Just like I did as a kid reciting Abe Lincoln's Gettysburg Address.

Speaking spontaneously is just the opposite; you forget little or no relevant information. You speak instinctively, from the heart, just like you'd speak in an everyday conversation. You don't need notes when you bump into a person and engage in a conversation, do you?

And if you do forget to say something, do you think the audience knows that? Do you think they go home and consider jumping out of a window because you omitted something in your speech? Of course not. They couldn't care less, and probably weren't even aware that you left something out.

The objective of my seminar is to train people how

to speak with few or no notes and crutches . . . to be as spontaneous, natural, and conversational as possible . . . and not to give canned, scripted talks.

Virtually every participant—whether an executive, middle manager, businessperson, or professional, or even a person with no public speaking experience at all—has mastered the techniques for giving spontaneous presentations with few notes and anxiety-producing crutches.

Even administrative assistants and technicians, who never have to speak publicly, have mastered the art of spontaneous speaking. It's simply more natural, instinctive, and visceral.

Victor Kand was a dynamic, intelligent young man who in a one-on-one conversation would win virtually everybody over. People loved him, trusted him, and adored his engaging, dynamic style of communicating.

But put Vic up in front of a group, and he would change into another person.

He'd get behind a podium, use a ton of notes, constantly look down at his script for dear life, and fail to make a human connection with his audience. His eye contact with the group was nil.

In short, when Vic spoke publicly, he was awful. His

good reputation as a hard-working, effective employee was undermined by his inability to give compelling oral presentations.

Vic was mandated to attend my High-Impact Presentations training program, and within two days of intense training and role-playing, was transformed into a dynamic, confident, self-assured spontaneous public speaker.

Like night and day. A dramatic change, all because he learned how to speak naturally and be himself up there, not somebody else. I admonished him to use this style in future and never go back to canned, stiff presentations. Once you learn the techniques for spontaneous speaking it's almost impossible to go back.

The rest of Vic's journey was amazing. Vic went on to become one of the company's most exceptional, compelling speakers. He built up an enormous following and support system, just because of his powerful, credible spontaneous speaking ability.

He went on, in the next thirty years, to positions at the top of the company, and when he retired, his farewell speech to some five hundred people was as poignant and impactful as any speech could be.

Stay away from the mistruth and bad advice of rehearsing it until you know it cold. Forget that! I don't want my Gettysburg Address experience ever happening to you. It traumatized me and I still feel the pain.

APPLYING THIS TO REAL LIFE

It might be a little risky to give more spontaneous, natural speeches or oral presentations, at least the first time or two you try.

But if you don't try, you'll never turn that bad habit and mistruth into a strength, and into a career and personal gain.

Canned, memorized, over-rehearsed, unnatural speeches must go. They're getting you nowhere, except into career growth trouble.

You've got to give spontaneous, natural, conversational presentations a chance. That's right. You have to give the presentation as if you're having an enlarged conversation with your audience. And they will appreciate this style and feel more engaged in what you have to say.

If the thought of this spontaneous speaking stresses you out, which is 100 percent normal, then start small and build gradually. That means . . . practice giving more spontaneous presentations to audiences you know very well, or even trusted friends, colleagues, or family. The risk is low with them.

As you begin to see that spontaneity works and it's the only way to go, then start to build the audience, build the challenge, and build your confidence.

Nothing builds confidence in public speaking more than going out and doing it frequently, receiving positive, specific feedback, and performing

without the use of distracting, ineffective crutches and painfully lengthy visual aids.

Eventually, you're going to find that much of the fear, anxiety, and trepidation is gone, although some discomfort and apprehension will always remain. That's quite normal, even for professional speakers.

The result: You'll be able to think better and more clearly on your feet when presenting. You'll be in more control of your subject matter, more in control of your audience and any distractions . . . and subsequently get better and better.

Once you gain that increased self-confidence, there's no stopping you with your public speaking, your formal and informal presentations. Having trained thousands of people globally over the years in spontaneous, high-impact public speaking, I have rarely seen a person not get it or not improve dramatically.

Yes, public speaking is one of the biggest phobias in the world, but no, it is not a challenge that can't be overcome. Tell yourself you're going to be yourself and speak the same way you do every day of your life, in an everyday conversation. And you're not going to rehearse it over and over again.

This will offset the advice of people who still promote old-fashioned tools, techniques, and outdated information on public speaking. It will turn the fears, anxieties, and tensions into communication excellence and credibility.

FLAXSEED FACTORS TO REMEMBER

1. You're kidding yourself if you think giving canned, over-rehearsed, scripted presentations is the way to go. This will not help you get to where you want to be, career-wise.

2. Giving dynamic, powerful, natural, and believable oral presentations, with no crutches that weaken your credibility, is critical to professional success and self-confidence.

3. "It's not just what you say . . . it's how you say it." A common and popular expression, especially with public speaking, but so true. Spontaneity is the only approach.

4. When you over-rehearse a talk, you sound like you're simply "giving a speech," and not sincerely and credibly presenting a powerful message from the heart.

5. Canned, scripted, over-rehearsed presentations can impede the believability and impact of any communication, and also hurt the dynamic, engaging, compelling nature of it.

6. Canned presentations that come across as scripted

can minimize or even eliminate the human connection between speaker and audience.

7. You don't need to rehearse it until you know it cold. Forget that! The normal stress and prespeech tension and butterflies can be channeled to produce high-impact, persuasive oral presentations.

8. Yes, it's a challenging skill. But yes . . . you and millions of other people can and will master public speaking and the fears and anxieties that emanate from having to give these speeches.

Eighteen

Lesson to Unlearn #18

Don't Use Your Hands When You Speak!

"Roger, do not speak with your hands," Miss Luzah, my eighth-grade public speaking teacher, repeatedly admonished me.

"It's not supposed to be done when speaking, and it's very distracting," she would say.

And when I'd retort by saying, "It seems to come naturally and it's hard to stop doing," she'd close-mindedly reject the statement and, coincidentally, vehemently gesture with her hands while saying it. Ha, ha!

"Don't use your hands when you speak" is another superficial, misleading lesson we were told as kids or early in our careers. Forget that! It's bad advice and can lead to career damage or something close to it. That's a pretty heavy statement, but I'll back it up shortly.

Yes, if you wave your hands constantly when you

speak, flailing them, it can become distracting and annoying to others. Some people get a headache because the hands make them dizzy. Others just get distracted by the excessive movement.

But there's a big difference between waving your hands and hand gesturing.

When you use your hands to gesture the points you're making, and emphasize them, you are accentuating them. You're showing your feelings and emotions nonverbally.

The key word is "effective," using your hands to help tell the story, paint the picture, demonstrate your enthusiasm and passion. This beats letting your arms dangle down by your sides, like they're atrophied or nailed to your hips.

Dinah Moe has strong opinions supported by factual examples and uses her hands and fingers to emphasize these points.

She'll use the count-off gesture when she's listing and enumerating things, raise her arms to show magnitude and breadth, and occasionally make a fist to demonstrate her unlimited support of an idea she espouses, or a program she believes in. Dinah makes her hands work for her, and they do.

She has a reputation for being a drop-dead motivational public speaker. Doing what my old speech teacher suggested would clearly reduce her persuasiveness and overall effectiveness.

Barney Booro has much to say but looks listless and comatose with his lack of animation and gestures. Sometimes people fall asleep when Mr. Booro is speaking.

I'll never forget that during one of his presentations, he was so boring that an attendee fell asleep and started snoring tumultuously. Sounded like thunder. Then he cut a loud one, totally asphyxiating the room. People cracked up and grabbed their noses. All this as Barney's arms remained down by his side like they were atrophied, debilitated, dead.

DATA BACKS THIS UP

You've probably seen the 7-38-55 Albert Mehrabian communication research, but if you haven't, let me review some important numbers: 7, 38, and 55.

Mehrabian's 7-38-55 rule is an internationally accepted communication theory that quantifies how much, at the beginning of a verbal communication, a person's initial impact is delivered via verbal and nonverbal communication.[16]

Shockingly, only 7 percent of what people initially communicate lies in their words. The rest of the message, at least at the outset of the communication, is conveyed through their tone of voice and body language.

That's right—38 percent of the speaker's initial impact comes from their effective voice, or lack thereof, and 55 percent comes from their body language, the hand and facial gestures that come with the words. I call this "The big 93 of communicating."

An example: Somebody asks you how your weekend went. You half-enthusiastically say, "It was fine." Your words say it was good, but everything else says something different. Or somebody asks you how the XYZ project went, and you say, "Pretty well," when in fact, your nonverbals and tone say, "It sucked."

Your hands and hand gestures are a major component of your body language and the nonverbal messages you intentionally or inadvertently send others. It's difficult to fake them unless you really try. They speak volumes, as does your eye contact, tonal and volume changes, and pauses.

When you speak publicly, lifeless hands and arms often show listlessness, low energy, lack of conviction, and little or no persuasiveness.

That eighth-grade teacher of mine told me that if I didn't stop using my hands so much, she'd tell my parents that I had a bad attitude and was difficult to teach. Say what? Get in hot water because of ineffective hand gesturing?

She probably read that information in an outdated book published a gazillion years ago. Very misleading and a clear mistruth.

FACT: If you don't gesture naturally with your hands, you tend to look stiff, nervous, tight, and undynamic. That is not helpful in developing your career and communication reputation as well as your organizational credibility.

APPLYING THIS TO REAL LIFE

There are many different hand gestures that help express your thoughts and ideas effectively.

Some of these gestures you do naturally, in everyday conversation or presentations. Others need to be learned and practiced.

Here's a simple technique that gets your hands moving in the right direction. It's called the ready position and is exactly what it implies. Put your hands in the ready position when you're about to begin presenting or speaking in a casual conversation.

The ready position means to keep your elbows tucked in at your sides, with your arms and hands out in front of you, and ready to gesture when the feeling comes to you.

Don't gesture just to look dynamic or cool. Gesture when the emotion of the message can be better delivered by the movement of the hands. When it comes naturally.

Hey—you do it in everyday conversation. And if you think you don't, take a look at your hands when you're at a cocktail party or meeting, and watch how they naturally gesture to accentuate your point. Watch other people and you'll see the natural and animated flow of the hands, for emphasis and accentuation of points.

And remember: You don't get a second chance to make a great first impression. The ready position at the beginning of an oral presentation helps prepare you to make that great first impression.

THE POWER OF YOUR HANDS: ELEVEN EXPRESSIVE HAND GESTURES

Try making your gestures purposeful, impactful, meaningful. Let them add emphasis to your key points. They should come across naturally and spontaneously.

Outstanding speakers synchronize their hand gestures with the major points they want to make, and the overall effect they want to have on the listeners. But they're cognizant of the fact that different cultures respond differently to hand gestures. Where one culture might be moved by a particular hand gesture, another culture might be turned off by it. For example, pointing with your index finger might by forceful and emphatic in the US, but it can be seen as being rude in China. So be wary of where you're presenting.

Here are eleven commonly applied hand gestures . . .

1. The **"Count-off"** gesture: When you're enumerating things, exhibit the corresponding gesture with your hands and fingers. It'll serve as a visual aid that will enhance listening and overall retention. It'll also keep you on track regarding where you are with your points.

2. **Clenched hand:** Making a fist will illustrate intensity and forcefulness of your point, without coming on too strong. Don't raise your voice or start yelling, which could come across as anger and irritation.

3. The **"Whole Thing"** gesture: Opening up your arms widely to indicate "everything" or "everywhere." This implies inclusiveness.

4. **"Thumbs up"** gesture: This communicates positiveness, supportiveness. But too much of this gesture can get old quickly and shouldn't be overdone. Some people use this each time they say hello or goodbye.

5. The **"Growing"** gesture: Moving your hand upward toward the sky indicates growth.

6. The **"Decreasing/Reducing in Size"** gesture:

Moving your hands downward signals the opposite of the "growing" gesture.

7. The **"Me, Personally"** gesture: Putting your hands on your chest says, "this comes from the heart."

8. **Forefinger pointing to temple:** This says, "I like that idea" or "That's a very interesting thought."

9. The **"Come together"** gesture: Bringing your two hands together. "We're one team!"

10. **Crossing fingers:** Communicates "Good luck" or "Let's hope this happens."

11. The **"Thank you"** gesture: Holding your hand upright with your fingers pointing upward, with your hand at the same level as your face, held for a second or two, conveys thanks.

These are just some of the many hand gestures you make, consciously or subconsciously. And most of them will eventually come naturally and spontaneously.

FLAXSEED FACTORS TO REMEMBER

1. Body language is a major part of communication. Effective, expressive hand gestures can embellish

that body language. When you're told not to use your hands when speaking, you're being advised to reduce the effectiveness of your body language. That is bad information. Forget that!

2. Use hand gestures naturally, emphatically, and spontaneously when speaking.

3. Begin your presentations in the ready position. Tuck your elbows in at your sides and have your arms and hands out in front of you, ready to gesture when you feel the urge to. Then speak and gesture naturally, as you would in everyday conversation.

4. Don't wave your hands all over the place like an orchestra conductor. But do use them to help make your points and illustrate your energy and enthusiasm.

5. Specifically, use your hands to show emphasis magnitude, drama, the emotion you feel, and to enumerate key points. Don't just flail them around.

6. There are numerous types of hand gestures. The eleven mentioned above are all geared to

complement your verbal communication with strong nonverbal messages.

7. Your body language is a major part of the first impression you make on others. Effective, expressive hand gestures enhance the first impression you make on people.

8. Remember Mehrabian's 7-38-55 rule. The first impression you make on listeners is heavily based on what you say nonverbally (55 percent) and with your tone of voice (38 percent). Only 7 percent of the initial first impression is based on your words.

9. You never get a second chance to make a great first impression.

Part Four
Maximizing Productivity

Consider this feeling . . .

"I'm swamped. I feel overwhelmed, overworked, spent, out of control. I seem to be always harried and juggling things and not getting nearly enough done. My feeling of not maximizing my productivity is stressing me out. I'm not sure what to do."

Have you ever felt like that? Stressed and stretched to the limit and feeling like you're not accomplishing nearly as much as you could and should. Living with deadlines that create tension and apprehension. Feeling disorganized and not fully in control of things.

In this digital age, maximizing productivity is discussed more than ever and is a key challenge and concern of millions. Books are continually being written about productivity, and people are constantly striving to gain more control over their work and lives.

One of the key factors in becoming more productive is getting a handle on things that directly or indirectly affect productivity. Things that create excessive stress and tension for you. This section focuses on four mis-truths that can negatively affect one's productivity.

Nineteen

Lesson to Unlearn #19

We Need to Conduct a Meeting

"Good morning. My name is Roger Flax. May I please speak with Mr. Antonio Gofredo?"

Response: "I'm sorry, Mr. Flax, but Mr. Gofredo is in a meeting."

Roger Flax again: "When will Antonio be free, ma'am?"

Response: "I'm sorry, but Mr. Gofredo, that's what we call him, has another meeting following his current meeting."

Roger again: "Oh, I see. Well, will he be in tomorrow, and if so, what time?"

Response: "No, Mr. Flax. He'll be out at an all-day meeting tomorrow."

Roger once again: "Hmm. How about Thursday, ma'am?"

Response: "On Thursday and Friday, he has

offsite meetings. Why don't you try him next week?"

Roger, disgusted: "Fine, I'll call him on Monday. What time is good for him?"

Response: "I just noticed he has back-to-back meetings all afternoon on Monday."

Roger: "Well, what about Monday morning?"

Response: "He's at a board scheduling meeting for the company golf and tennis outing."

Roger: "Then can I have his cell phone number and try calling that number?"

Response: "Mr. Flax, I cannot give out his cell number to anybody unless he authorizes that."

Roger: "Thank you, ma'am. And be well!"

How many times has that happened to you? You try getting somebody on the phone and it's impossible, totally unrealistic. And beyond frustrating.

How many times have you tried reaching somebody, but you're told that they're at a meeting?

Meetings have become the incurable curse at organizations. Seems like everybody's at a meeting.

HOW, WHY, AND WHEN TO SCHEDULE A MEETING

Before you think of scheduling or attending a meeting, first ask yourself several relevant questions.

1. Do I really need a meeting?

2. Can the meeting be done via another method?

3. Who needs to attend the meeting? And why?

4. If the CEO of the organization said that you can't conduct a meeting unless it borders on life or death, what would you do instead?

5. If you couldn't schedule the meeting in two weeks, and you felt it was urgent, what would you do?

WHEN AND WHY MEETINGS ARE IMPORTANT

Now that you think that I despise meetings and think they are, for the most part, worthless, let's see why that thought is untrue.

Meetings can be important, but there are just too many of them. You should conduct them carefully and selectively.

Studies have found that in-person teams generate 15 to 20 percent more ideas than virtual ones,[17] while fully remote employees are 10 percent less productive.[18] And a *Harvard Business Review* survey showed that 95 percent of people feel face-to-face meetings are much better in ensuring longer, more productive relationships among people.[19]

That alone tells you why in-person meetings can be essential. Meetings do often result in more collaboration and creative thinking. But scheduling weekly meetings to update matters when there's not much to update is a waste of time.

WHEN SCHEDULING A MEETING IS NECESSARY: RULES TO FOLLOW

1. Decide whether the meeting is absolutely necessary. Ask yourself . . . is there any better way to accomplish the objectives of the meeting? If not, then schedule it.

2. Regardless of the type of meeting—a short team meeting, a brainstorming session, or a problem-solving / strategic gathering, establish the objective of the meeting and let all participants know what it is.

3. Determine an agenda for the meeting and send it out at least three days in advance.

4. Let people know in advance their role in the meeting and what prework needs to be done by them.

5. Set goals and desired outcomes for the meeting.

Let these guide you in conducting and steering the flow of the meeting.

6. Decide on the best vehicle or setting for the meeting. Would online be sufficient or is it wisest to get people in the same room? Each has its pros and cons, so weigh these factors before deciding.

7. Start on time. The two-minute rule says that you'll wait ONLY two minutes maximum from the official starting time before commencing the meeting. Don't penalize people on time just because a straggler or two is holding up the meeting. Begin punctually.

8. Be a facilitator for the meeting. Get everyone to participate. If somebody is silent, ask them a question to initiate their involvement.

9. Don't permit dominators to take over the meeting. When somebody is controlling, jump in and get others to participate more.

10. Don't embarrass people who are incorrect or blatantly wrong in a point they make. Instead, suggest you and that person meet afterward for a few minutes to further discuss the item.

11. End on time. Stick closely to the agenda and required timeframes for each item. Let people know at the outset what each agenda item is, and how much time is allocated to each area.

12. Be firm and decisive in leading the meeting. This is a time to show effective leadership.

13. At the conclusion of the meeting, sum up the action points and what each participant needs to do as follow-up.

14. Thank the people for attending and end with a motivating comment.

15. Gain feedback on the meeting. Send a brief email to each attendant asking for input on how they felt the meeting went. Do this for each meeting and you'll learn if your meetings are productive.

APPLYING THIS TO REAL LIFE

I apologize for sounding like a lecturer but the lesson to unlearn here is simple: Meetings steal people's time, and if you must conduct them, make them productive.

Follow the fifteen steps above and pat yourself on the back if you've conducted a productive, beneficial, action-oriented meeting.

I personally conduct very few meetings, but when I do, I'm tough on myself to make them worthwhile. You be the same.

FLAXSEED FACTORS TO REMEMBER

1. Review the fifteen points made above.

2. The key point to remember: Do you truly need the meeting? If we did not conduct the meeting, what would we do to attain the same results?

3. Be critical with yourself: What are we doing differently based on the meeting? Did we really need it? If so, great. If not, learn from this.

4. Conduct fewer meetings than ever. Have fewer participants, only those truly necessary. Spend less time in meetings, if at all possible.

5. Meetings can be a key component in organizational communication but can also be a big waste of time and hinder everyone's productivity.

Twenty

Lesson to Unlearn #20

Stress Is Bad for You

How totally false that premise is! It's a myth. Incorrect. Forget that!

Anybody who tells you that stress is bad for you knows little or nothing about stress and stress management. Ask them where they learned that stress is bad for you. Silence will ensue.

Stress, as a rule, isn't bad for you. It's part of a full, energized, productive life.

It's the bad stress, or distress, that is bad for you.

First let's look at how stress is defined and then see how stress, when managed correctly, is not necessarily bad for you.

Stress, according to *Merriam-Webster's Collegiate Dictionary*, is "a physical, chemical, or emotional factor that causes bodily or mental tension."[20]

Wikipedia describes stress as "a feeling of emotional strain and pressure. Stress is a type of psychological pain. Small amounts of stress may be beneficial, as it can improve athletic performance, motivation, and reaction to the environment. Excessive amounts of stress, however, can increase the risk of strokes, heart attacks, ulcers, and mental illnesses such as depression, and also aggravation of a pre-existing condition."[21]

There are countless books, articles, definitions, and interpretations of what stress is. But one thing is for sure: Stress is part of life, and we all have it. Some denialists claim they have no stress in their lives. Say what? Are they Martians?

It's not whether we have stress. We all do. It's how we manage stress that matters.

Sure, too much stress in your life, and not managed or channeled properly, can be detrimental to your health. Can even lead to cardio, neuro, and other health-related problems. And it can be psychologically frightening for some folks who fear that stress will kill them.

But without any stress at all, where would we be? Probably dead, or on the way.

Stress is normal and part of a healthy, dynamic life, personally and professionally. We all experience it, and it goes hand-in-hand with the challenges of living and surviving.

Show me a person who says they don't have stress, and I'll show you a liar!

Don't think that you must remove all your stress—it just won't happen. Learn how to deal with stress, manage and channel it. If you don't know how, take a course or seminar in stress management, as it could be a life changer. Or seek professional advice to reduce excess stress.

But don't ignore it, especially when you feel overwhelmed by it.

TWO TYPES OF STRESS

There are two types of stress: Eustress (which you've probably never heard of) and distress, something we often hear about or feel much too much, especially with what's been going on in the world.

Eustress is good/positive stress. *Merriam-Webster's Collegiate Dictionary* defines it as "a positive form of stress having a beneficial effect on health, motivation, performance, and emotional well-being."[22]

Examples are getting married, the holiday season, a big vacation coming up, a major promotion or accomplishment at work, an important presentation coming up, the birth of a child.

With eustress, feel-good endorphins are released. These endorphins, according to MedPark Hospital in Bangkok, are "neurotransmitters released by the pituitary gland and hypothalamus in the brain. As natural hormones, they can alleviate pain, lower stress, improve mood, and enhance your sense of well-being."[23]

That kind of stress is healthy for you and can result in more productive, channeled energy. It's invigorating. Feels good. But eustress can also wear you down and must be managed.

Distress, on the other hand, is bad/negative stress. The website MentalHealth.com gives examples such as being fired or laid off, filing for divorce, a death in the family, injury, a heated argument, hospitalization, dirty organizational politics, having a jerk as a boss. Or when your business is in a slump . . . or your proposal fell short and was rejected.[24] The list of examples is endless, and distress can be as simple as a traffic jam on the highway or bad weather on vacation.

That type of stress is not good for you. It's draining. It can be debilitating. You should face it and proactively manage and methodically reduce it. I'll review how to do that in a few moments. But first, an interesting tidbit of information . . .

Renowned Harvard psychology professor and international best-selling author Dr. Tal Ben-Shahar sees stress as a potential self-fulfilling prophecy, a "prediction a person makes that causes itself to be true, due to the behavior of the believer."

The highly acclaimed professor, who is known to

have taught Harvard University's highest-rated course ever, believes that . . .

"If you see stress as bad, catastrophic, and something you need to avoid at all costs, each time you get stressed, it's going to have a very negative effect on you."[25]

Dr. Ben-Shahar also concluded that if you see stress as something that can make you more resilient, you will experience it more effectively. It can be a real positive in your life.

FACT: Channeling the stress into positive experiences and engagements can give you the impetus and drive to accomplish more and be more successful. It can be a motivator.

Two stress channeling examples stand out vividly in my life. I'm proud of one but the other still gives me agita.

Proud, Uplifting Example: I was playing in a national platform tennis tournament against the number one ranked senior platform tennis doubles team in the USA. My partner and I were anxious and stressed-out about the match, playing these three-time national champions. There was no way we could beat them, at least we thought.

We split the first two sets—each team won a set, and the match went to a third set and eventually a twelve-point tiebreaker. That's like overtime in other sports. Man, were we feeling the tension and stress! I felt my knees shaking. But it was energizing and cool.

I told my partner, Jonathan Scott, that we had

nothing to lose, everything to gain—because these guys were national champions and we were club players. They were more stressed-out and tense than we were because the pressure was on them, I whispered.

So, we channeled the stressful circumstance into an energized high emotion, grunting and groaning with each point, mini set—the tiebreaker. The stress made us play better and at a higher level. We were so pumped from the emotion created by the stress that we lifted our level and upset them, 13–11.

That stress was good for us—eustress—and it made us perform better. Our opponents probably had distress, playing two turkeys, whom they should have decimated in two straight sets.

Traumatic, Debilitating Example: I had to recite a poem in grade school called "Oh Captain! My Captain!," and we were told by the teacher to memorize, rehearse, rerehearse the poem at home until we knew it cold. I went over it again and again with my mom and dad. Rehearsed it in the shower, in the car, in bed. I knew it perfectly by the night before, as I rehearsed it one final time.

As I got closer and closer to the big performance, I got incredibly tense. The stress of possibly forgetting lines grew exponentially.

Then came the big day—presenting that poem in front of my classmates and teacher. I was beyond stressed-out—I thought I was going to have a heart attack.

So, distressed, frightened, and anxious about the poem, I panicked minutes before I was called on, completely froze, and forgot the opening lines.

The stress caused my knees to shake, my heart to pound, and my armpits to flood with sweat. When I was about to say the words, "Oh Captain! my Captain! our fearful trip is done," I inadvertently said . . . "Oh Captain! my Captain! our fearful *tit* is done," and the class went bonkers with laughter. The teacher reprimanded me and threatened to throw me out of the room for using a "naughty" word.

That inability to properly channel the stress was bad for me; it froze me up and made me feel temporarily brain-dead. I couldn't think on my feet at all. To this day, I think of that enormously distressful, exasperating experience.

MANAGING YOUR STRESS

How do you deal with your distress, or negative stress? Several relaxation, or "ReFlaxation," steps follow . . .

1. **Identify and admit it.** Face the fact that you are feeling stressed about something, bad or good. Don't make believe it doesn't exist. Holding it in is the worst thing you can do. Some people

repress and ignore it . . . this is a terrible and potentially dangerous habit.

2. **Recall and identify the specific causes** of the stress. What incident, situation, or person has stressed you? Take time to give it serious thought. Why did it happen? Does it happen frequently, personally or professionally? What caused it to happen, precipitated it? Who or what does it occur with? Where? Why?

3. **Face and accept the stress.** It's becoming part of your life. Determine what needs to be done, now or soon, to eliminate the stress or substantially reduce it. Take immediate action.

4. **Learn and grow from it.** Sit back and think about what caused that stress, how it might have been prevented. And do everything possible not to ever let it happen again.

TOOLS TO REDUCE STRESS

To reduce stress or the tension that emanates from it, consider doing the following:

Take several deep, cleansing breaths . . . close your eyes, breathe four or five times through your nose . . . then exhale slowly . . . mumbling the number one, then the number two, and through the number five. Think about something different from the item that's stressing you. Lose yourself in your thoughts. Let your mind escape from the reality you're in at that moment.

Another stress reduction technique that works for me: I try taking a bike ride when I'm feeling major negative stress. Somehow, it feels better or less stressful after the ride. (Except my butt always hurts with those hard bike seats.) Focusing on safety during the ride gets my mind off what's been stressing me out.

In the winter, when it's too cold to take a bike ride, I try working out on a treadmill or bike machine. There are many other physical exercises to reduce the strains of excessive stress. One of them is swimming, or if you're not a swimmer, treading water and hand paddling.

If the stress is created by something that keeps you up at night or represents a challenge that you can't get a handle on, disconnect and walk away for a while. If it's 3:00 a.m. and you still can't sleep, take a short strut in your home.

I turn on soft, mellow music that has no lyrics, and that usually gets me right back to sleep or slowly relaxes me. Or I mentally count sheep: "Thirty-three beautiful white sheep grazing in the grass, with the hot sun shining on them." And then I repeat the same sentence but with thirty-two beautiful white sheep, etc., and down to twenty-nine sheep. By then, I feel myself drifting away. Incidentally, when trying to fall asleep, I intentionally keep my eyes open for as long as possible, and they suddenly close themselves as I'm on the way to sleep. Try this if you're having difficulty falling asleep.

The key is to stop thinking about your problem, whatever and whenever it is. Do something else, and eventually go back to the problem and focus on solving it, or even remove yourself from it.

FIGHT OR FLIGHT

Once again, realize that not all stress is not bad for you. It's part of life and is never going away, regardless of who you are. But it can be managed effectively and channeled into energy and vigor, if you put your mind to it.

Yes, stress is often called "the silent killer," but rid yourself of the thought that all stress is bad for you. Forget that!

It's part of a normal, productive life, and it is manageable. And in many instances, it's energizing and propelling. But don't deny it—fight it or "fly away." The fight-or-flight response is a protecting reaction that is critical to our physical survival, especially when we're in a precarious, frightening situation.

APPLYING THIS TO REAL LIFE

Stress is serious business. Understanding it better can be beneficial.

Don't let it overwhelm you and get out of control. Get a handle on it immediately. Most people are aware of it, but don't proactively manage it or make stress management a priority in their lives. They hope or believe that it will eventually go away.

According to the American Psychological Association, "chronic stress, which is constant and persists over an extended period of time," can contribute to long-term problems for heart and blood vessels.[26]

The consistent and ongoing increase in heart rate, the elevated levels of stress hormones, and the high blood pressure that can result can all take a toll on the body.

Stress affects all systems of the body including the musculoskeletal, respiratory, cardiovascular, endocrine, gastrointestinal, nervous, and reproductive systems. Our body is equipped to handle stress in small doses, but when it becomes long-term or chronic, it can have serious effects on your body.

As a starter to get a handle on your stress, consider the following routine . . .

1. Keep a notebook regarding every time you feel stressed, tense, anxious, angered.

2. Summarize what incident caused those stressful feelings.

3. Describe how you felt—physically, emotionally, psychologically.

4. Who is the trusted person in your life that you could share these feelings or emotions with? Identify that person now.

5. Follow up with that person you trust and respect to discuss it.

6. What were the lessons learned from the experience?

7. What would you do differently next time to avoid the bad stress, or distress, that you experienced?

8. Try to enhance the good stress and engage in more activities that produce it. You'll be much more productive for it!

Remember: Stress is not bad for you. In many instances, it's actually good for you and energizing in many ways. Make stress reduction and channeling stress a part of your everyday lifestyle if you haven't already done so.

Don't let stress get out of hand and manage you. Instead, manage it proactively.

FLAXSEED FACTORS TO REMEMBER

1. Beginning today, adopt a lifestyle that incorporates stress reduction and healthful living. Get into the habit and routine of using these stress management tools and techniques every day of your life.

2. Make a list of the specific things that stress you out or create tension and anxiety. Prioritize the stressors in that list—the A's, life-or-death health issues; the B's, serious issues like family, business, or personal problems; and the C's, the nagging problems, nuisances, mundane, annoying irritants.

3. Try not missing one day of stress reduction, "ReFlaxation" exercises, tension control, auto-suggestion/breathing tools. Relax with Flax! Try getting a good deal of exercise every day.

4. Make stress management a major priority in your life—as mentioned, it can be a silent killer if not managed regularly. It should be as important as any other activity in your life.

5. Remember . . . not all stress is bad! Eustress (the good stress) is wonderful for you and can increase your productivity.

6. The bad stress, the distress, needs to be managed, reduced, and ultimately eliminated.

7. "Fight or Flight!" Fight the stress proactively or flee from it. But do something about it!

Twenty-One

Lesson to Unlearn #21

Don't Multitask—Stay Focused on One Task at a Time

The concept of multitasking has created much confusion and huge differences of opinion.

Even the definition of multitasking is controversial. It means different things to different people. And the research on it varies widely.

Picture being given this advice from somebody . . .

"Stop multitasking! Focus on one thing at a time, and get it done right. Don't move on to something else until you are completely finished. Multitasking causes mistakes."

That person simply doesn't get it. Or is rigid. Or living in the past. Maybe thirty or forty years ago, that was the case. Seems like people "outlawed" or bad-mouthed multitasking then.

But today's a different ballgame. There's a different

set of priorities, challenges are greater, agendas are constantly changing, there are multiple ways to communicate, social media has created new kinds of connections, etc. People claim they're more jammed, more crazed, than ever.

Employees at all levels, top to bottom, are being inundated by an ever-increasing influx of tasks, duties, shifting priorities, crises, puzzles to solve, problems to resolve. Ever since digitization became enormously prevalent, it changed the world. And it's changing every week.

Not to multitask, as a cut-and-dry rule, is bad advice. Or very risky, at best. Forget that!

In addition to being a fallacious premise, that mistruth can be counterproductive and a major time waster. Why? There are times when multitasking absolutely must occur; otherwise, you won't get the task(s) completed. Or, if completed, not done on time.

Me? I can't live without multitasking. That's been the case since I was a kid. I was always in a hurry to get things done quickly so I could go have fun. So, I multitasked.

And with interruptions, changing priorities, and so much going on, I often went from a task to a chore to a challenge, and back to the first task . . . and actually didn't mind that style. Never got bored. It felt productive. And somehow, I'd get it all done.

The degree of multitasking is different for different people. It depends on their personality style and how busy they are. But we all need to multitask at times, if not frequently.

Multitasking is actually a good habit, a key skill when you want to maximize your productivity in the allotted time, and get the work done well. However, there is good and bad multitasking, effective and ineffective. The good, effective multitasking should be part of your life routine. The bad, ineffective, should be quelled immediately.

GOOD AND BAD MULTITASKING

Whether or not a certain activity is considered multitasking is often a matter of subjective perception—the same activity may or may not be perceived as multitasking. And some of that activity is "switchtasking."

Yes, it's a bad habit when you start one thing, then go to another, and subsequently jump to a third and fourth task, then return to the second task, etc., before you've completed the first task.

That's an unproductive way to get things done quickly and efficiently. Research backs that point up—when we try doing two or three things at the very same time, we are less efficient and more prone to errors.

And if people call that multitasking, and suggest you curtail it, they're correct. Avoid it.

The key words are "the very same time." We humans can't do two or three things at the very same time.

Constantly having to focus and refocus can drain your time and energy, which impacts your overall performance and productivity. That's what some of the experts say. Stanford University researchers frighteningly found that multitasking "kills your performance and may even damage your brain."[27]

A study by the University of London found that "participants who multitasked during cognitive tasks"—i.e., tasks that require a person to mentally process new information, acquire and organize knowledge, and allow them to recall and retrieve that information from memory and to use that information at a later time in the same or similar situation—"experienced IQ score declines similar to what they'd expect if they had smoked marijuana or stayed up all night."[28]

Some of the multitasking subjects had their IQ drop fifteen points, falling to "the average range of an 8-year-old child."[29]

Pretty shocking. IQ decreases fifteen points? Almost hard to believe.

Yes, there's a "growing body of research that shows that multitasking actually decreases productivity, impairs your cognitive ability, increases your stress, and diminishes your creativity."[30] All these things, according to some authorities, can make you less effective and dramatically reduce your overall professionalism and productivity.

Focusing on more than one assignment at a time, repeatedly switching back and forth between two or more activities, or performing a number of unrelated tasks in rapid succession can all be considered multitasking. Experts say that our minds simply are not wired for this type of overload.

The performance of the human brain, according to some studies, breaks down when it attempts to engage in two tasks that require conscious thought at the same time.

I respect people who say you should never multitask, but they're usually not meaning multitask. Doing one thing that forces you to focus intently, then out of nowhere, doing another thing, unrelated, while thinking of the first thing. Then going back to the first thing . . . then taking a call, etc.

I don't call that multitasking. I call that out-of-control freneticism, being frantic and in a constant craze.

Research has found that there may be benefits to multitasking. Dr. Chaitali Kapadia, assistant professor at Florida International University's College of Business, and professor of organizational behavior Dr. Shimul

Melwani stated that . . . "Multitasking creates a greater demand for cognitive resources, such as attention and working memory. Our brain activates more resources to meet those increased demands. Once our brain achieves a higher level of activation, it can use that extra energy in different ways because of cognitive flexibility." The research suggests that how we design and schedule our work can impact outcomes we care about, such as creativity.

They say, "we can be more balanced in how we think of our multitasking," not multitasking with "detail-oriented work that [you] have to be careful with." But "if you know that you're going to be doing something that's a little bit more creative, then getting yourself energized through multitasking, taking care of some of those other tasks, might be helpful."[31]

"Everybody multitasks," Dr. Melwani says, "and we're made to feel bad if we admit to doing it." She adds that "This research gives us that little bit of flexibility to say, 'There are some tasks I have to be careful about, but there are also benefits to multitasking.'"[32]

Then there's the research conducted by Rom Schrift, associate professor of marketing at Indiana University, along with doctoral student Shalena Srna and Yale professor of marketing Gal Zauberman, who found that . . . "multitasking is a mere illusion because it is impossible to execute more than one task at a time. Nevertheless, the perception of multitasking seems to be beneficial to performance."[33]

The general concept of multitasking tends to be misconstrued by people. Some people are brainwashed and convinced that you should never multitask, period, the end, because they've heard that advice for years, and haven't really challenged it. Never multitask? Forget that!

Think about it. There are "brainless" things you can do simultaneously without diminishing performance, like folding laundry and speaking on the phone, taking out the garbage and planning your day, or making a bed and thinking about a proposal you must deliver. Your mind is on autopilot when doing some things.

When I am swimming laps each day, my mind is on anything but swimming. Many of the lifeguards tell me that they feel brain-dead, watching people swim laps all day while their minds are a million miles away daydreaming about something else.

When I take a long walk, I multitask by getting important phone calls over with. I can still keep my mind on where I am and where I need to turn.

The key thing to remember is doing things that

require complete focus and thought will suffer in quality when multitasking.

GOOD MULTITASKING DEFINED

When you're working on more than one task during the same general period of time, you're invariably saving time while accomplishing your overall objectives. While multitasking, you're not compromising or minimizing the overall effectiveness and efficiency of the work.

It can also be described as making every second count. Not wasting any time. Excellent time managers are terrific at that. They don't waste a moment.

When you take a shower and plan your day, or rehearse your upcoming big presentation, or try to solve a problem that's challenging or haunting you, you're, in essence, multitasking.

Many of my clients multitask with me when they're driving to and from work. They'll call me on the way home, for example, a forty-five-minute drive, and we'll speak for forty-four of those minutes. Of course, they have to drive home anyway, so those forty-four minutes of commuting and communication didn't really take a second. They had to be driving anyway. A gift of time.

Me, personally? If I didn't multitask every day, I wouldn't get many of the things done I must get done for people. Simply wouldn't—there's not enough time in the day or week.

—

Take Seymour Axshun, for example. Seymour is always multitasking . . . but he is on top of everything he's doing and is tuned in to achieving top quality and results.

He will take a long walk, say around one hour, while doing some mental problem-solving about a potential crisis, challenge, or proposal that's on his mind. And he'll take his dog on the walk, and even call a person or two during the hour.

He'll often preschedule a business or personal call or two during that walk. He stretches his arms and shoulders while walking and talking. Carries a smartphone to text himself important ideas that come to him. He's doing much more than just walking, and he's optimizing his time in the process. Vintage multitasking at its best.

Seymour has done an hour's worth of work and gotten in an hour of exercise. Multiply that by many days a year, and he's maximizing his time management and productivity while exercising. He's saving hundreds of hours in the process.

By multitasking and doing these things during his long walk, in essence the time for the walk is on the house.

It's actually consuming zero minutes. That's because he's getting an hour's worth of work done that needs to be done sooner or later, during that same period of time.

When Seymour does "no-brainer" things like folding clothes or carrying things into and out of the house, he sometimes tries getting in a short phone call or two, if necessary.

He sometimes sets up walking meetings with associates to discuss issues and get exercise at the same time. Some people do that already, but they don't do it enough. That's a form of multitasking.

Walking meetings accomplish two things: People can discuss problems, brainstorm issues, or accomplish other things, and can get some exercise at the same time. Walking meetings lend themselves to nice, social interactions between colleagues, versus what might happen in a potentially tense, conference-room setting.

A one-hour walk can represent two hours of productive time utilized, if multitasked.

While on hold during a call, Seymour will do something productive during the dead time, like texting a few reminders to himself, or typing or reading emails. We live in a world of ongoing customer service department delays. For whatever reason, we often wait what seems like forever with boring, canned music playing, and intermittent recorded messages asking us to "please hold for a few moments." That occurs until the recordings end and the live person gets on the line. Seymour expects to be put on hold, so he prepares work for that time waster. It all adds up.

I once called a hospital and was put on hold for fifteen minutes. Thank goodness it wasn't life-or-death. I spent the time writing a few emails.

Before any call to a company or organization, preplan another task or two to perform while waiting. Assume you'll be put on hold.

A client of mine uses the microwave oven a lot during the day, for food, reheating coffee, defrosting things, etc., whether working remotely from home or in the office.

Instead of standing by the microwave waiting for the task to be completed, she'll multitask—do some leg stretching, clean some dishes (at home), or even head to the restroom. Time is a person's biggest asset, and she's obsessed with making the most of it, so she has more time for other work, family, and fun.

I try to walk four to five miles a day. Walking everyday can get old and boring.

So right before each walk, I plan what I need to get

done during this walk, whether it's a client call, a proposal I'm planning to write, a problem that needs to be solved, a poem I want to create, or just a phone call to friends or acquaintances that I can never find the time to call.

I don't just walk and do nothing else. Multitasking during one- to two-hour walks has become a major time-saver for me, and a way of life. Multiply that by 365 days a year and you can see why.

These are examples of good multitasking—accomplishing several things in a certain amount of time—rather than just taking a walk, or sitting worthlessly and unproductively while on hold, or waiting around as a one- or two-minute function or task is being taken care of.

BAD MULTITASKING DEFINED

Bad multitasking often occurs when you're in the middle of something, and you permit interruptions or distractions, and you let yourself change directions. That's a time waster and detrimental. Research has shown that switching back and forth from one task to the other can reduce productivity and efficiency as much as 40 percent.

Being in the middle of some serious, creative thinking and suddenly stopping, and starting something else . . . and then going back to the first thing is totally unproductive. Or working on two or three important proposals at a time, going from one to the other. Get the first one done, then move to the next.

Working on a report or on something important with the television on is bad multitasking. Some people can do this, but they're in the minority. Most people end up wasting more time than they realize. Ditto news blasting in the background, especially when so much is bad news. That's a time waster.

REMEMBER: One of the major keys to effective multitasking is planning.

Prior to beginning any task or activity, think about other things you might have to do soon, just in case you are detained, or put on hold, or delayed, or find yourself with several minutes of unproductive time.

Limit the number of things you multitask or juggle to two or three. Discipline yourself to spending a minimum of twenty uninterrupted minutes on something, without allowing a single distraction.

Shifting from one task to another makes it difficult to tune out those distractions and usually creates mental blocks that will slow you down or cause unnecessary errors. It also takes time to get your mind and thinking back on track. So, forget that!

In sum, there's effective and ineffective multitasking. Make effective multitasking part of your life.

APPLYING THIS TO REAL LIFE

First, give the whole area of multitasking some thought. We covered several examples so perhaps reread them. Think about how, in the past, you have done multitasking well, or not so well.

Remind yourself of the difference between monotasking (performing one task at a time) and multitasking.

Think of times when you could have multitasked and didn't. And think of times when you did multitask, and it was a distraction and productivity diminisher.

Then begin to multitask whenever it makes sense.

Keep a record of the increased productivity you experience during multitasking. Pat yourself on the back and keep it going.

FLAXSEED FACTORS TO REMEMBER

1. Multitask whenever you can, as long as the quality of everything you're multitasking is not diminished. If it is, don't take on that second or third task.

2. Most activities that require active attention cannot be done simultaneously.

3. Multitasking is a matter of subjective perception. People see it in different ways, with different applications, different benefits, different risks. But

thinking that multitasking is unproductive and should be avoided is a mistruth.

In the allotted time you have for a particular task, and if your multitasking won't negatively affect your productivity or overall quality, don't allow any wasted time. Make every second count. If you can accomplish two or three things in the same allotted time, do it.

4. Effective multitasking especially applies when calling a person or a company over the phone and being put on hold. Or sitting in a doctor's waiting room. Or sitting in traffic. Or doing a task where you must stand nearby as things get done.

5. This includes being on a lengthy, boring conferences or Zoom calls with many other people, where you've got to be on, but really have no role . . . or shouldn't be on in the first place. This also applies to exercising, walking, daydreaming, and just chilling.

6. The key to effective multitasking is planning in advance. This includes "downtime" planning when there might be a lull or delay.

7. You'll be amazed at how much more you can get done in downtime—simple or everyday things

that eventually have to get done—if you plan those things in advance. The saving of time will quickly add up without you even realizing it.

8. Most people multitask but are often made to feel bad about it. Don't be one of them. A multitasking frame of mind is a productive frame of mind.

Twenty-Two

Lesson to Unlearn #22

Say Yes When You Possibly Can

Who hasn't gone through this painful scenario?

Saying yes to a person who requests something when the real answer should unequivocally be no, but something is holding you back from saying that two-letter word.

"Yeah, Kenny, I'll try getting it done although I'm incredibly busy right now. But I'll get it done somehow."

Forget that!

You just created more stress for yourself. You didn't want to disappoint Kenny or come across as standoffish. You jumped through hoops to do what you should have said no to because you simply didn't have the time. And by the way, other things that you needed to get done suffered because of your inability to just say no.

This lesson to unlearn is for people working with

other people and trying to please and not disappoint them. The lesson is for CEOs, presidents, and other leaders who aim to please people, and not disappoint or let them down. It also occurs at home—with spouses, kids, family, friends.

It happened to me recently when I told a buddy and his wife I'd be at their shore house in an hour. He had asked me to get there by noon for brunch with his family and friends, and I said OK. That was a pretty ridiculous task on a holiday Sunday morning, especially since that day the infamous Garden State Parkway was bumper to bumper a third of the way and it took us over ninety minutes to get to his home. Why didn't I just say, "Gonna be tough, but I'll get to your place as soon as possible."

The fear of saying no is an awful habit to get into and often causes a great deal of unnecessary stress.

Brad Denning, who knew he wanted to fix and repair cars at the age of six, has one of the biggest hearts you'll ever see. He owns Dobbs Auto Body, an auto body shop in New Jersey, and is the go-to guy if you have a serious problem with your car. That's the good news, but the bad news is that Brad told me that he has a difficult time saying "No, I can't get it done now" to his customers.

He loves his clientele, but when they demand that he get to their car immediately, he acquiesces and accepts that unreasonable request. And that inability to just say no causes him and his team nothing but unneeded stress. They get the job done on time, but the stress and tension it creates is debilitating to Brad and enormously stressful to his talented team.

Forget that bad habit, Brad. You'll live longer . . . and the job will get done anyway!

WHY THIS HAPPENS

As kids, we were conditioned not to say no for a variety of reasons.

The main one was that we didn't want to disappoint the person asking for something even though we knew that saying yes would create a new set of problems. One of those problems was that you'd be taken away from what you should have been doing at that time. Or you'd fear you'd be disappointing the person and might someday pay the penalty for not saying yes.

I remember as a kid often trying to please people and promising them things I had no time to spend on. And then being annoyed with myself for not getting done what I needed to do immediately. I wasn't strong enough to just say no for fear of hurting their feelings or pissing them off.

When I started my company at a fairly young age, I always tried to be nice to everybody and not say no to requests. And then I would pay for those nonassertive, foolish responses later on.

This may be Assertiveness 101, but the "learn to say no" problem has existed for many years for some people and has hurt them in different ways. One of these ways is that they often misprioritize things that have to get done when they don't have the time to do them all. They get into trouble and pay the price dearly.

WHY PEOPLE HAVE DIFFICULTY SAYING NO

There could be many reasons.

As a kid, perhaps saying no to your parents would get you in trouble.

As a student, you wouldn't say no to a teacher for fear they would get you back, punish you for "back-talk," or give you a lower grade.

If you said no to a dear friend, perhaps you would offend the person or possibly lose their friendship.

You might be a people pleaser who goes through life trying to make the other person happy.

Somebody very near and dear to me did that the first ten years of their life, and when they realized what they were doing, reversed themselves 180 degrees and started pleasing only themselves. (Doing something in between those two extremes might have been healthier.) They realized, "If you don't please yourself, whom do you really please?"

There are political reasons why some people say yes when no is the only correct answer. They're concerned that no might hurt their career and the perception others have of them. How silly, but true for many political animals in organizations. At work, saying yes when no should be the answer is a good way to hamper productivity.

In the field of politics, many politicians say yes to people when they know no is the answer. That's why many people avoid going into politics; it's sometimes hard to tell the truth.

THE BIG DECISION, YES OR NO . . . AND HOW TO DECIDE

Whether it's at work or at home, ask yourself several basic questions before you say yes to something you should be saying no to.

*First and foremost, do you have the time to do this? This is a simple question that must be honestly faced and answered. Be completely frank with yourself.

*Do you have the energy to do it now, or are you spent and exhausted and don't have the zest to do it, at least now?

*Are you saying yes just to please the person and score some goodwill or brownie points?

*Is there something more important you must do right now, versus what you're being requested to do?

*How long will this request take you, and what other priorities do you have?

*What's the major downside of saying no? Any

politics involved? Any possible career derailers? Any feelings hurt?

*What, if anything, do you fear could happen if you say no? Worse-case scenario?

*If you do this task now, will you get the other priorities you have completed on time?

*Thinking back, what was your initial mental response when asked to do the task?

***And finally, what does your gut tell you? People might lie but the gut never does. This should be the first thing you ponder—your gut reaction to the request.**

APPLYING THIS TO REAL LIFE

I know this is just one of twenty-two lessons to unlearn but it ranks with the most important ones. Being non-assertive could cause mental problems that affect other decisions you make.

Here's a quick eight-step process to master the art of learning to say no when no should be the answer . . .

1. Take mental note of what your gut feeling is regarding the request. Is it a yes, no, or "let me first give it some thought"? There's nothing wrong with letting a person know that because you're so jammed, you need a little time to respond and will get back to them shortly.

2. Ask specific, relevant questions regarding the task requested or anything else that is being required of you.

3. Find out what the exact timeframe is. How long will this take me?

4. On receiving that timeframe, tell the person what you're presently doing, how time-consuming this work is, the completion deadline for the work, and other items which would support a no decision.

5. Measure the upside risks versus downside risks of agreeing to yes.

6. If the answer is no, explain why and try giving an alternate response which might be satisfactory (like performing this task later in the day or first thing tomorrow, etc.).

7. In essence, say no to the request, not the person.

8. Read their reaction, verbal and nonverbal, and if necessary, respond to those signals immediately. You certainly don't want to offend them.

9. End on a positive, either way.

The benefits of unlearning the fear of saying no are many. It's good for your health and sanity, good for your effective time management, good for your career in the long run, and good for your feelings of personal productivity, well-being, and assertiveness.

Like everything else, you've got to want to do this. It's not difficult to adhere to if you truly want to adopt this assertive behavior. Get in the habit of being as resolute as the other person is pushy.

I started adopting this assertive behavior many years ago and swear by it as an important life skill and time-saver. It changed my life, and it'll change yours. I never looked back.

FLAXSEED FACTORS TO REMEMBER

1. Just say no when no is the best and most logical answer.

2. If no should be your response, and you feel bad about that, don't let guilt permeate you. In the short and long run, you are doing the correct thing.

3. The communication process for saying no goes like this . . .

   *Get right to the point and say, "No, I'm sorry, I can't do that at this time." That should be stated up front and early, and not in a wishy-washy way.

*Give factual, supportive reasons why you can't do it now.

*Briefly tell the person what the negative impact of saying yes would be for you and/or your organization.

*Offer an alternative solution to their request.

4. Keep your voice low and facial expressions sincere when responding.

5. Follow up with the person to ensure they know when you will have the time to deal with their request. Jot it down.

6. Saying no when a person needs you for something is never easy. But it's an important behavior to apply. And it's mentally healthy to adopt the "no is the answer" habit when it is appropriate. It's unhealthy to say yes and kill yourself trying to accomplish it on time.

Twenty-Three

Tying It All Together . . .

Be the Best You

"You cannot teach an old dog new tricks" is an old, popular, still-used expression. You've heard it many times before, I'm sure.

I don't buy that old adage at all, because that's all that it is—an outdated, worn-out saying that simply doesn't fit anymore in the fast-paced, dynamically changing world we live in. Forget that!

Yes, it's got some validity for some people, especially people dead set in their ways or totally unmotivated or uninspired.

But it's not true for most of us. In fact, it's hogwash. If you don't keep up with the changing times and new technologies, you're lost!

When the slogan was created, there were no such things as social media, digitization, or computers.

There was nothing close to the enormous amount of change that takes place every week and every day in this vibrant, unpredictable twenty-first century.

FACT: You can change behaviors and old ways of doing things if you put your mind to it and see the value. It's all in your head.

Although some lessons learned from childhood or young adulthood are harder than others to unlearn, you can definitely learn to overcome them. Getting them out of your system permanently is the goal, but you must want that change.

Everyone's experience is different. But one thing is consistent—many of the things we've been taught over the years are so incorrect and faulty that unlearning them is essential. That's what this book has been all about.

Remember, this whole thing is not psychotherapy, rocket science, artificial intelligence, or high tech. It's self-improvement awareness and training, and striving to be the very best you that you can possibly be.

You don't need to "fix" yourself because you're not broken or damaged. But you do need to self-actualize and feel that you're continuing to grow as a person. That goes for all of us.

It might take some introspection, trial and error, and patience to unlearn some of the lessons taught to you years back. But perseverance will go a long way in effectuating new behaviors; new skills, habits, and concepts; and updated tools and techniques. In sum, further excellence.

Eventually, these mistruths will dissipate into cyberspace and the new lessons learned will come naturally. And in time, your new behaviors and skills will become second nature.

Here are several things to ponder and follow up on, to make this learning experience a life-changing one. Give them a shot . . .

1. **Internalize within yourself.** Have an internal self-conversation soon and decide which of these lessons you want to focus on. Then make a commitment to follow up and go for it.

2. **Think about the pros and cons** of adopting each recommended change, as described in each chapter.

3. **Think big, but execute small**, or in smaller pieces. You don't have to tackle the whole item at once and expect immediate results. Gradually build up the momentum of accepting the particular change

and what you need to do to effectuate it, bring it about, and make it reality. Once you succeed in the smaller task or thought, move on to the next one, until you attain the desired result.

4. **Be energized, optimistic, and upbeat** about dealing with the potential lessons to unlearn. Change is exciting and a major aspect of life.

5. **Find a way to implement the change**, and if practice is needed, set that time up soon and go forward. If you put this off, you might never get to it, and eventually, what you read will dissipate.

6. **Partner with a mentor.** It's not a bad idea to find a mentor or confide in somebody you know well and trust and let them know what you're doing. Their frankness, feedback, and candor about you and your newly acquired knowledge can only be a positive, in the short and long run.

7. **If some of your areas of change are work-related**, why not discuss with your manager what you're doing and how it can have a positive effect on you and your work. Of course, some of the things you will work on are very personal and have nothing to do with work. So, keep them inside.

8. **Reward yourself** when you implement or try out your newly acquired skills, tools, techniques, behaviors, or beliefs. Treat yourself to something special.

9. **Throughout all this, keep your cup half full not half empty.** Positiveness breeds excellence.

10. **If appropriate, share some of these learnings with friends, colleagues, employees**, any people who mean a lot to you and could benefit from hearing about the new you.

I look forward to hearing from you regarding how you're tying these new ideas into your professional and/or personal life.

Please keep in touch with me at roger@horizon-edge.com if you want to share any experiences with me, or if you have questions or challenges you want to communicate. I welcome hearing from you 24-7 whenever you need or want to connect.

That's it for now, my friend. Let's tie as many of these lessons unlearned to your next action steps as a person who's looking to be the best you. And remember the general principle of "forget that," when, in fact, that is the correct answer.

Thank you for your time, and best of luck.

BE WELL . . .

Roger

CONTACT INFORMATION:

Roger Flax, PhD

Peebs Horizon, LLC

Roger@Horizon-edge.com

Acknowledgments

Thank you to:

My family—Judy, Charlie, Jonny, Kenny—who every day, subtly or not so subtly, intentionally or through osmosis, teach me meaningful things about life . . . who we are, what is family, and what our real purpose truly is. More than you know, guys.

To my late parents, Dr. Charles and Shirley Flax, who, like millions of other wonderful parents in this world, taught valuable lessons to me that stuck for my entire life . . . as they dedicated their entire lives to helping and healing people.

To my sister, Ronni, who along with me learned so many life lessons from Mom and Dad, and whose courage and commitment in her life challenges are ongoing and heartfelt.

To my wonderful clients, whom I've loved working with, some for over forty years . . . and whose careers, lives, successes, and challenges are so important to me.

To my dear friends—you know who you are—who are fun to be with, fun to learn from, and fun to mutually bust chops, nonstop.

To my incomparable sixth-grade teacher, Catherine "Katy" Lynam, who constantly drilled into my head what effective communication was about, and that I should always follow my dreams and go for it.

To Anthony Goff, innovative and dynamic president of Blackstone Publishing, who took a shot, publishing my first book, *No Stopping You! How to Win the Game of Life*. You're an inspiration, AG, in my goal to continue writing compelling, upbeat self-improvement books that benefit, develop, and motivate people to reach their fullest potential. Get your rocket first serve in more!

To Janet Cooke, Blackstone's outstanding book publishing consultant and a wonderful person who helped fine-tune and further develop *Forget That!* and hugely exceeded my expectations. What a great pleasure working with you, Janet.

To Johnson & Johnson, the very first company that let me in the door as a consultant several decades ago . . . to train, coach, and eventually mentor their biggest assets, their employees. What an honor working with this wonderful, credo-driven company that has such an enormous healthcare impact on people throughout the world.

And to you, my readers, who have invested your time (in me) to read this book. I appreciate you guys a ton and welcome hearing from you after you have read the book and applied some of the newly acquired ideas.

I mean this sincerely . . . how could I ever do it without all of you?

About the Author

Dr. Roger Flax built one of America's most successful leadership development consulting firms. He has conducted thousands of seminars over decades for 400+ organizations in five continents. He is the creator of **Building Character for Life**, an experiential character development program for children ages seven to twelve, and the **Horizon Talent Developer™**, a digitized program that gives leaders and high potentials feedback on how they're perceived in twenty-one leadership, interpersonal, and communications areas versus how they perceive themselves in these areas. He now licenses and customizes this digitized web-based coaching/mentoring program for companies and profit and nonprofit organizations. Roger has worked with numerous executives; professionals in sales, marketing, finance, and technology; corporate general counsels and lawyers; political figures; professional athletes; and he has developed training programs applicable to a variety of fields and levels of management.

He is the author of *No Stopping You! How to Win the Game of Life*, available from Blackstone Publishing and distributed internationally. His latest book, *Forget That! 22 Lessons You Must Unlearn to Succeed*, was published by Blackstone Publishing in April 2025.

A globally known consultant in leadership, communications, and presentations coaching, Roger has impacted millions through radio and TV interviews; training seminars and keynote speeches; newspaper, magazine, and online articles; and worldwide corporate conferences. He has appeared on CBS, ABC, Fox, and CNBC, and his work has been published in *USA Today*, *The New York Times*, *The Wall Street Journal*, *Bloomberg Businessweek*, *Forbes*, *Barron's*, Bottom Line Inc., and *Fortune*.

Roger was a well-known tennis pro who helped the University of Maryland achieve an ACC Championship and top-ten NCAA ranking. His twenty Eastern Tennis Camps trained 12,000+ players. He has won over fifty tournaments and consistently placed highly throughout his career. He is also a self-taught pianist and guitarist, and he has written songs released by Atlantic Records, Vanguard Records, Mercury Records, and Golden Records. Roger co-wrote and executive produced the films *The Last Home Run* which was featured on HBO, and *30 Days* starring Taye Diggs, Hill Harper, Charlie Neal, and Ellen Burstyn.

His many clients have included: Johnson & Johnson, *USA Today*, IBM, PepsiCo, Nabisco, Medtronic, Citibank, Reebok, AT&T, the Charles Schwab Corporation, Bank of America, Boston Scientific, Kraft, Levi Strauss & Co., L'Oreal, Mars Inc., Simon & Schuster, JPMorgan Chase & Co., Pfizer, the New York Stock Exchange, Bristol Myers Squibb, Prudential, Guardian Life, Pharmacia, United Airlines, Equitable, Atlantic Health, SmithKline Beecham, Novo Nordisk, Endo International, and American Express, among others.

Roger received a bachelor's degree from the University of Maryland; his master's and Ph.D. degrees are from The Catholic University of America. He is married to Dr. Judy Flax, a former associate research professor at Rutgers University and a specialist in language-based learning disabilities and autism. They have three sons.

Endnotes

Chapter 3

1. *The Kid Stays in the Picture*, written by Robert Evans and Brett Morgan, directed by Nanette Burstein and Brett Morgan (USA Films, 2002).

Chapter 4

2. Merriam-Webster's Collegiate Dictionary, s.v. "fact," accessed October 1, 2024, https://unabridged.merriam-webster.com/collegiate/fact.

Chapter 5

3. Merriam-Webster's Collegiate Dictionary, s.v. "confidential," accessed October 1, 2024, https://unabridged.merriam-webster.com/collegiate/confidential.

4. Merriam-Webster's Collegiate Dictionary, s.v. "secret," accessed October 1, 2024, https://unabridged.merriam-webster.com/collegiate/secret.

Chapter 6

5. Les Brown (@thelesbrown), "Shoot for the moon.... even if you miss, you'll land among the stars!!" Facebook, November 30, 2013, https://www.facebook.com/thelesbrown/posts/shoot-for-the-mooneven-if-you-miss-youll-land-among-the-stars-its-better-to-aim-/10152008461834654/.

Chapter 7

6. Alvin Toffler, *Future Shock*, (Bantam Books, 1971, originally published in 1970 by Random House), pg. 414, https://archive.org/details/FutureShock-Toffler/page/n429/mode/2up?q=illiterate.

Chapter 10

7. "Save It For A Rainy Day," BookBrowse.com, https://www.bookbrowse.com/expressions/detail/index.cfm/expression_number/576/save-it-for-a-rainy-day.
8. Merriam-Webster's Collegiate Dictionary, s.v. "frugal," accessed October 2, 2024, https://unabridged.merriam-webster.com/collegiate/frugal.

9. Merriam-Webster's Collegiate Dictionary, s.v. "cheapskate," accessed October 2, 2024, https://unabridged.merriam-webster.com/collegiate/cheapskate.
10. Merriam-Webster's Collegiate Dictionary, s.v. "spendthrift," accessed October 2, 2024, https://unabridged.merriam-webster.com/collegiate/spendthrift.
11. Merriam-Webster's Collegiate Dictionary, s.v. "miser," accessed October 2, 2024, https://unabridged.merriam-webster.com/collegiate/miser.

Part 3

12. Merriam-Webster's Collegiate Dictionary, s.v. "communication," accessed October 2, 2024, https://unabridged.merriam-webster.com/collegiate/communication.

Chapter 14

13. Merriam-Webster's Collegiate Dictionary, s.v. "reprimand," accessed October 2, 2024, https://unabridged.merriam-webster.com/collegiate/reprimand.

Chapter 15

14. "Take it or leave it," BookBrowse.com, https://www.bookbrowse.com/expressions/detail/index.cfm/expression_number/417/take-it-or-leave-it.

Chapter 17

15. Abraham Lincoln, Gettysburg Address, Bliss Copy, November 19, 1863, accessed through Abraham Lincoln Online, https://www.abrahamlincolnonline.org/lincoln/speeches/gettysburg.htm.

Chapter 18

16. "How Much of Communication is Nonverbal?" The University of Texas Permian Basin, https://online.utpb.edu/about-us/articles/communication/how-much-of-communication-is-nonverbal/.

Chapter 19

17. Melanie S. Brucks and Jonathan Levav, "Virtual communication curbs creative idea generation," *Nature* 605, 108–112 (2022). https://doi.org/10.1038/s41586-022-04643-y.
18. Don Lee, "Remote workers actually aren't more productive. Will bosses finally call them back in this year?" *Los Angels Times*, January 4, 2024, https://www.latimes.com/business/story/2024-01-04/2024-year-employers-clamp-down-on-remote-work-not-so-fast.
19. "Managing Across Distance in Today's Economic Climate: The Value of Face-To-Face Communication," *Harvard Business Review*, April 20, 2016, https://hbr.org/resources/pdfs/comm/british-airways/hbras_ba_report_web.pdf.

Chapter 20

20. *Merriam-Webster's Collegiate Dictionary*, s.v. "stress," accessed October 14, 2024, https://unabridged.merriam-webster.com/collegiate/stress.
21. "Psychological stress," Wikipedia, https://en.wikipedia.org/wiki/Psychological_stress.
22. Merriam-Webster's Collegiate Dictionary, s.v. "eustress," accessed October 3, 2024, https://unabridged.merriam-webster.com/collegiate/eustress.
23. Thitiporn Supasitthumrong, "Endorphins: The 'feel good' chemicals for well-being," MedPark Hospital, https://www.medparkhospital.com/en-US/lifestyles/endorphins.
24. "Types of Stressors (Eustress vs. Distress)," MentalHealth.com, updated September 25, 2024, https://www.mentalhealth.com/library/types-of-stressors.
25. Kate Branch, "Why Experts Are Suddenly Saying Stress is a Good Thing," *Vogue*, December 18, 2018, https://www.vogue.com/article/stress-anxiety-positive-psychology-happiness-health.
26. "Stress won't go away? Maybe you are suffering from chronic stress," American Psychological Association, updated November 1, 2022, https://www.apa.org/topics/stress/chronic.

Chapter 21

27. Travis Bradberry, "Multitasking damages your brain and career, new studies suggest," *Forbes*. October 8, 2014, https://www.forbes.com/sites/travisbradberry/2014/10/08/multitasking-damages-your-brain-and-career-new-studies-suggest/.
28. Bradberry, "Multitasking damages your brain and career, new studies suggest."
29. Bradberry, "Multitasking damages your brain and career, new studies suggest."
30. "The Multitasking Mirage," University of Florida, https://training.hr.ufl.edu/resources/LeadershipToolkit/transcripts/multitasking_mirage.pdf.
31. "Need a creativity boost?" News & Stories, University of North Carolina Kenan-Flagler Business School, September 10, 2020, https://www.kenan-flagler.unc.edu/news/need-a-creativity-boost/.
32. "Need a creativity boost?"
33. Knowledge at Wharton Staff, "The real (and imaginary) benefits of multitasking," Knowledge at Wharton, Wharton School of the University of Pennsylvania, December 26, 2017, https://knowledge.wharton.upenn.edu/article/real-imaginary-benefits-multitasking/.